THE GREEN EDGE

HOW SUSTAINABILITY CAN POWER YOUR BOTTOM LINE

Publishing the Voice of Southern Appalachia

BENJAMIN WORLEY

Disclaimer

The views, opinions, and interpretations expressed in this book are solely those of the author and do not necessarily reflect the views of any companies, organizations, or individuals mentioned herein. While every effort has been made to ensure the accuracy of the information provided, this book is for informational purposes only, and the author assumes no responsibility for errors or omissions.

The mention of specific companies, products, or organizations does not imply any affiliation or endorsement by those entities, nor does it intend to imply any form of defamation or harm. The inclusion of real-world examples is for illustrative purposes and does not reflect any official involvement with or endorsement of the companies or organizations mentioned.

This book should not be considered legal, financial, or professional advice. The reader should consult appropriate professionals before making any decisions based on the content herein.

Book Cover by Benjamin Worley

ISBN: 9798345212219

First edition 2024

For the farmers

TABLE OF CONTENTS

1.   So There I Was
2.   How We Got Here
3.   We Should Be Worried
4.   State of (in)Action
5.   The Case For Farmers
6.   The Impact on the Rest of Us
7.   The Nitty Gritty Dirt...Stuff
8.   Show Me the Money
9.   Prove It
10.   But, But, But...
11.   A Way Forward
Appendix: Case Studies
Bibliography

1
So There I Was

Every good story I've ever been told starts the same way: So, no kidding, there I was. Let's not break tradition here. So, no kidding, there I was, the summer of 2022, knee-high in a rice paddy in Central Thailand. Now, this isn't the 'beautiful sun kissed beach with towering rock formations' Thailand or the 'majestic temple adorned mountaintop' Thailand. This is the 'flat, paddies as far as the eye can see' Thailand. And it's hot. It's always hot in Thailand, but the summer is the worst. The humidity is through the roof and any outdoor exertion inevitably ends in the need for a cool shower and a change into dry clothes.

But business necessitated that I put myself in the middle of that rice paddy in the dead heat of summer so I could talk with Saowanee, a lovely rice farmer from Suphan Buri province. Saowanee is a slight woman, middle aged, with luxurious straight black hair and one of those infectious smiles for which the Thai people are so well know. She has been a rice farmer her entire life, coming from a long family of rice farmers in a traditional rice farming district. My point is, she knows a bit about rice, and I feel we can trust her judgement when it comes to running the farm.

I was in Thailand to learn more about the effects of climate change on the region's farmers, specifically the smallholder farmers who make up more than 80% of the agricultural production in Southeast Asia. That's more than 100 million people in the region, or roughly 40% of its workforce. Yeah, that's right…40%. For those who don't know, a smallholder farmer is defined by the UN Food and Agriculture Organization (FAO) as:

"Smallholders are small-scale farmers, pastoralists, forest keepers, fishers who manage areas varying from less than one hectare to 10 hectares. Smallholders are characterized by family-focused motives such as favouring the stability of the farm household system, using mainly family labour for production and using part of the produce for family consumption." [1]

In my experience, smallholders tend to fall on the lower range of that scale, landing somewhere under 2 hectares. But a more important part of the definition than size, is the use of primarily family labor and keeping a portion for family consumption. In fact, globally, the approximately 500 million smallholder farms produce about 35% of the world's food. In regions like Sub-Saharan Africa and South Asia, that number is even higher, approaching 50%. For many of these communities, farming is not just a job; it's their entire way of life.

My reason for talking to Saowanee, other than because she was a charming person, was to get a firsthand account of the impacts of climate change on her farm. At the time, my company was looking to implement a program to engage smallholder farmers in positive climate action. But before we did that, we really needed to know just how big of an impact, if any, climate change was having on their operations. What I discovered was unsettling.

Many of the issues Saowanee and I discussed were

to be expected. The heat was noticeably increased, not just in terms of absolute temperature, but in duration. One example she gave was that growing up, she and her family could easily work for most of the day out in the paddies with only a minimal break for a midday meal in the shade. But in recent years, those breaks have become more frequent and the ability to continue working at peak productivity has declined significantly. Obviously, this is anecdotal, and the reduced productivity could be attributed to several things. After all, I can no longer hop out of bed without worrying I'll slip a disc like I could when I was in my twenties. But as I interviewed more farmers who all said the same thing, the trend was hard to ignore completely.

And it wasn't just the heat. The weather patterns have become more erratic, which has wreaked havoc on her ability to plan. She showed me the logs she's kept over the years recording many of her farm activities. In the past, she could predict with some certainty when the monsoon rains would come, allowing her to time planting and harvesting with precision. But now? She laughed—a short, mirthless chuckle. "Now, I plant and pray," she said. The rains come too early some years, making the process of field preparation and seeding extremely difficult, or they arrive late and leave the young rice plants struggling for water. More than once, she's lost an entire crop to unpredictable storms or prolonged dry spells.

According to the UN FAO, erratic rainfall and prolonged dry spells in Southeast Asia have led to decreased agricultural productivity and increased crop losses. Farmers in Thailand have reported shifts in monsoon patterns, resulting in challenges with irrigation scheduling, increased water stress, and more frequent flooding events[2]. Research by the Southeast Asian Climate Consortium found that over 70% of surveyed farmers in Thailand reported that they could no longer predict the start and end of the monsoon season with the same accuracy as in previous decades. This has led to delays in planting and increased use of irrigation, further straining resources [3].

It's not just water availability that's changed. The soil, which used to hold moisture more reliably, has become less predictable as well. The once fertile earth has turned patchy, with some areas becoming prone to waterlogging and others drying out too quickly. This has forced her to buy additional fertilizers to keep yields up. But the price of fertilizers has skyrocketed in recent years. Global supply chain disruptions, increased fuel costs, and production issues have all contributed to the increased price. What used to cost her 1,200 baht now costs nearly double. And even when she can afford it, the quality is inconsistent. Sometimes the fertilizer is potent enough to burn her crops; other times, it's too weak to make much of a difference.

And the yields? Let's just say that consistency has gone out the window. Some years, her rice plants flourish despite the challenges, producing almost as much as they did a decade ago. But in other years, she's barely breaking even. "It's like a lottery," she told me. "One year you're comfortable; the next, you're scrambling to pay off debts." And it's not just yield variability—global rice prices, which had been relatively stable since the 1980's, have experienced significant fluctuations in recent years. What she used to sell at a stable price now sees sharp increases and decreases, making it impossible to budget accurately or plan for the future.

The unpredictability has introduced financial stress not only for her but for the entire community. Saowanee shared stories of neighbors who, faced with shrinking margins and increased debts, have had to sell off parts of their land or, worse, leave farming altogether. In its examination of the economic and environmental vulnerabilities of Southeast Asia related to climate change, the Asian

Development Bank (ADB) highlighted that unpredictable weather patterns have forced many smallholder farmers to adopt coping mechanisms such as reducing crop diversity and increasing use of expensive inputs like fertilizers to compensate for lower yields. This has led to increased debt and financial insecurity among farming communities[4], a problem that was already a major issue before the effects of climate change exacerbated it. This isn't just a loss for their families; it's a loss for the local economy and the broader food supply chain. Every farm that goes under means fewer rice paddies producing food, fewer opportunities for seasonal workers, and more families on the brink of poverty. Many formerly productive fields now lay fallow, owned by Bangkok-based families. The situation became such a problem that, in 2019, the government passed a law expanding the tax rate on unused properties to discourage land hoarding and encourage agricultural production.

And the ripple effect doesn't stop there. When farmers can't grow as much or must sell their crops at a loss, they have less money to spend in the local economy. "People stop going to the markets," she explained. "They don't buy new clothes. They cut back on everything." What starts as a poor harvest ends up depressing the entire local economy. Multiply that by hundreds of communities, and you're looking at a massive economic downturn.

The more we talked, the more it became clear: for Saowanee and millions of farmers like her, climate change is not some abstract future threat. It's a present reality, one that affects their crops, their finances, and their very way of life. Yes, farmers worldwide (and I've talked to thousands of them), just like most of us, seem to enjoy complaining about things. And many of these smallholder farmers in SE Asia are no different. But it's hard not to take their complaints seriously when so much is seemingly at stake.

By the end of our conversation, we were both drenched

in sweat (admittedly I had perspired significantly more), and I had a notebook full of bleak observations. As I thanked her for her time, she smiled again—genuine this time—and said, "If you can help, please do. If not, at least tell people what's happening."

So that's what I'm doing here. No kidding, there I was, in the middle of a rice field, wondering if the world really understood what's at stake.

The real Saowanee

2
How We Got Here

The Birth of Agriculture: Settling Down and Growing Up

If there's one constant in human history, it's that we all have to eat. And we all eventually die. And we have to sleep, too. Come to think of it, there are actually a ton of constants throughout human history. But eating is for sure, way up there on the list. And while our methods of obtaining food have evolved—starting with the hunter-gatherer days, transitioning through the advent of agriculture, and landing us in the era of supermarkets that boast year-round blueberries—the basic need remains the same. But the way we've organized ourselves to satisfy that need? Well, that's a whole different story.

Let's rewind a few thousand years. Agriculture as we know it—planting crops and domesticating animals—got its start about 12,000 years ago in the Fertile Crescent, which, for those a little rusty on their geography, includes modern-day Iraq, Syria, Lebanon, and parts of Turkey. At that time, people began to realize it was far more convenient to stay in one place, grow some wheat, and keep a few goats around than it was to chase down dinner every night.

This aligns well with the Laziness Theory which posits that people will inherently look for shortcuts and quicker methods to complete a task in order to minimize effort. Although farming is by no means an easy vocation, it beats the pants off of getting into a foot race with gazelles every day. Settling down allowed societies to develop and populations to boom, and pretty soon, we weren't just growing enough food to get by. We were growing enough to create surpluses. And with surpluses, some people could focus on things other than farming—artisans, merchants, priests, rulers, and social media influencers (those Sumerians really knew how to make a great cat meme).

Over the centuries, agriculture developed hand-in-hand with societies. The plow allowed for faster, deeper tilling; crop rotation and selective breeding improved yields; and the integration of animals like oxen for plowing made cultivation a bit less back-breaking (for the human, anyway). This early innovation, though incremental, laid the groundwork for the societies that eventually built the pyramids, charted the stars, and, much later, argued over zoning laws and organic labels.

Industrialization: Farming at Scale

Fast forward to the 18th century, when everything changed. The Industrial Revolution—the era of steam engines, railroads, and cities choked by coal smoke—had a profound impact on agriculture. New machinery like the seed drill and mechanical reaper revolutionized the speed and efficiency of farming. Suddenly, a single farmer could plant and harvest many times the amount of food they could before. But that's not where the changes stopped. This period also marked the beginning of large-scale, mechanized farming. The first whispers of what we now call industrial agriculture were heard, though it was still a far cry from the factory-farmed meat and monocultured cornfields we think of today.

Industrialized agriculture didn't just change the landscape—it redefined rural economies and labor patterns. Mechanization displaced millions of rural workers, pushing them into cities and altering the social fabric of nations. Rural populations dwindled, and the agrarian way of life that had sustained humanity for millennia began to fade. Meanwhile, agricultural production boomed, laying the groundwork for urbanization and modern industrial economies. This shift transformed the relationship between people and the land, turning farming into a commercial enterprise rather than a way of life.

The Green Revolution: A Double-Edged Sword

Agriculture was no longer just a family affair—it was a business. A business that benefitted immensely from the next wave of changes in the early 20th century, which we lovingly call the Green Revolution. No, not that kind of "green." This one was named for the massive increases in crop yields sparked by new technologies, synthetic fertilizers, pesticides, and high-yield crop varieties. In a little over 30 years, starting around the 1940s, countries like India and Mexico doubled, even tripled, their food production. Norman Borlaug, the agronomist credited with spearheading this revolution, is often said to have "saved more lives than anyone else in human history" through his work in developing these technologies; credited with saving more than 1 billion people from starvation. 1 billion! Makes me a little less proud of that one time I saved a lost dog on the side of the road. For his efforts, he was awarded the Nobel Peace Prize, Presidential Medal of Freedom, and Congressional Gold Medal. Personally, I think Dr. Borlaug's name should be as well-known as Isaac Newton, Albert Einstein, and Mahatma Gandhi for his impact on the world.

Plus, none of those three ever made it into the National Wrestling Hall of Fame, but guess who did? Yep, Norman.

So, what's not to love? We solved hunger, right? Well, sort of. While the Green Revolution brought food security to millions and fed the rapidly growing post-war population, it also set the stage for a new set of problems. The success of these methods made industrialized, input-heavy, and monoculture-based farming the global norm. Practices like intensive irrigation, heavy use of chemical fertilizers and pesticides, and reliance on just a handful of crop varieties became widespread. These approaches, while wildly successful in increasing short-term production, broke the traditional relationship between humans and the land and were the start of agriculture's rocky relationship with the environment.

The Role of Policy: Incentivizing Industrial Agriculture

It wasn't just technological innovation that fueled the rise of industrial agriculture; government policies have played a major role in shaping today's global food system. In the United States, for example, farm subsidies have heavily favored commodity crops like corn, wheat, and soybeans since the 1970s. By providing financial assistance to farmers for these specific crops, the government ensured their steady production, which in turn lowered prices and made these ingredients ubiquitous in the food supply. Corn, in particular, became the backbone of countless processed foods and the primary feedstock for livestock, contributing to the rise of monocultures and intensive animal farming. The intent was to protect farmers from volatile market fluctuations, but the consequence has been an overproduction of these crops at the expense of crop diversity, soil health, and small-scale farming.

Similarly, India's Minimum Support Prices (MSP) were introduced to guarantee farmers a stable income and encourage the cultivation of staple grains like wheat and rice. While the MSP has helped prevent food shortages and supported rural livelihoods, it has also created significant environmental issues. The guaranteed price structure has driven many farmers to over-rely on water-intensive rice cultivation, even in regions with scarce water resources. As a result, groundwater levels have plummeted, and soil salinity has increased, leading to a host of long-term environmental challenges. Additionally, the focus on a few staple crops has crowded out more diverse and climate-resilient agricultural practices, making Indian agriculture more vulnerable to the impacts of climate change.

By prioritizing production and economic stability through subsidies and price supports, these policies have unintentionally reinforced the very practices that contribute to environmental degradation and climate vulnerability. While they succeeded in providing food security and economic stability in their respective contexts, they also set the stage for a system that is now grappling with sustainability issues on a global scale.

Modern Agriculture: Boon and Bane

You see, nature doesn't like to be pushed around. Just ask that stubborn patch of non-grass in my front yard (*Dear HOA, I'm working on it*). As we've forced the land to yield more than it naturally would, we've disrupted ecological systems, degraded soils, and drained aquifers faster than they can replenish. And these disruptions had a ripple effect on other natural systems. Soil degradation, which often results from over-farming and reliance on chemical fertilizers, reduces the soil's ability to retain water. This leads to increased runoff and erosion during heavy rains, while during dry spells, crops struggle to access the moisture they need. The end result is lower crop resilience and greater dependence on artificial irrigation systems which can then lead to even more chemical runoff. And the more we did it, the more we needed to keep doing it. What started as a tool to feed the hungry became a dependency that, like any addiction, is proving hard to quit. If you're thinking this sounds like borrowing from Peter to pay Paul, you'd be right. And now Paul's come knocking—he's wearing a *"climate change"* t-shirt, and he's not happy. He's also sporting a man-bun, but that's neither here nor there.

Since the mid-20th century, global agriculture has become a driving force behind environmental degradation and climate change. Synthetic fertilizers, which made crop yields soar, also led to a massive increase in nitrous oxide emissions, a greenhouse gas that's about 300 times more potent than CO_2. Nitrous Oxide is great at the dentist, not so much in the atmosphere. Heavy irrigation has depleted water tables, and overuse of pesticides and herbicides has polluted rivers and soils, killing off beneficial organisms and creating resistant pests and diseases. The loss of biodiversity in agricultural landscapes disrupts natural pest control mechanisms. When only a few species are grown in monocultures, pests that feed on those crops can thrive unchecked, necessitating more pesticide use. This, in turn, kills off beneficial insects and further reduces biodiversity, creating a vicious cycle of pest management challenges. Then there's deforestation—cutting down rainforests to make way for pasture and farmland—responsible for nearly 20% of global carbon emissions. Industrial-scale animal agriculture, particularly cattle farming, has added methane emissions, another potent greenhouse gas, to the mix.

The global food system, as a result, has become one of the biggest contributors to greenhouse gas emissions, deforestation, and biodiversity loss. Yet, it is arguably the most vulnerable major industry to the very changes it has helped create. And it's more fragile than ever. We've built a system that's optimized for short-term yield and efficiency at the expense of long-term sustainability and resilience. So, while the Green Revolution fed billions and made modern society possible, it also planted the seeds (pun very much intended) of our current crisis. Critics argue that the Green Revolution's reliance on chemical inputs set the stage for today's environmental woes. But perhaps this is less a critique of Borlaug and more of how we've failed to build on his work in a sustainable way. Dr. Borlaug himself noted that there was no silver bullet to fix all problems and that the solutions must continue to evolve. Regardless of your view, it is impossible to make an argument that we would be where we are as a civilization today without the contributions of the Green Revolution.

Looking Forward: New Paths for Agriculture

But that's not the end of the story. Agriculture, with all its problems, remains the backbone of human civilization and the key to addressing climate change. The modern era has seen the rise of innovative farming practices aimed at reversing some of the damage—sustainable and regenerative agriculture, agroforestry, integrated pest management, and organic farming to name a few. Take agroforestry, for example. By incorporating trees into their fields, farmers in the Sahel region of Africa have managed to restore soil fertility, combat desertification, and increase their yields—all while sequestering carbon. Yet, despite these local successes, practices like these remain underutilized in the global agricultural landscape.

Globalization and Smallholder Farmers: Struggling to Keep Up

Yet, there's a catch. As we've globalized our food supply chains, these more sustainable practices remain the exception, not the rule. Global trade policies, subsidies, and market incentives still favor the industrialized, input-heavy models of farming established during the Green Revolution. And smallholder farmers, who produce a third of the world's food, are often excluded from these innovations altogether because of limited access to resources, knowledge, and markets. Which brings us back to where we started—in a rice paddy in Thailand, talking to farmers like Saowanee, who are trying to navigate this complex web of tradition, market pressures, and a rapidly changing climate.

Wrapping Up: How Did We Get Here?

So how did we get here? Through a few thousand years of incremental changes, a couple of revolutions, and a lot of good intentions paving the way to a pretty unsustainable system. Fixing it won't be easy, but it's possible. After all, the same ingenuity and persistence that got us to this point might just be the thing that helps us find a way forward.

The environmental and economic issues we face today in agriculture are not merely byproducts of farming but are deeply rooted in decisions made over centuries to prioritize short-term gains and efficiency over long-term sustainability and resilience. In the next chapter, we'll move beyond history and dive into what's happening right now. From falling crop yields and farmer bankruptcies to rising food prices and global instability, we'll explore how climate change is already disrupting agriculture worldwide—and why this should worry all of us. Because if there's one thing we can all agree on, it's that we don't already have enough things to worry about.

3
We Should Be Worried

When it comes to climate change, we're often inundated with phrases like "unprecedented times" and "record-breaking heatwaves." But those phrases can feel abstract, especially if they only pop up as a scrolling headline during your morning coffee. They make for good soundbites but don't really capture the complexity of what's happening. So, what do these terms actually mean for the people who grow our food, manage our water resources, or ensure that our cities don't get swallowed by rising seas? It's easy to get lost in the jargon and even easier to become desensitized to the urgency behind it. So, let's break it down: climate change isn't just raising the temperature a notch or two. It's rewriting the rules of our natural world, and that affects everything.

Think of it like this: when we talk about climate change, we're not just talking about warmer summers. We're talking about longer and more intense droughts, devastating floods, and unpredictable storms that tear through communities like a wrecking ball. We're talking about a higher likelihood of extreme weather events that are capable of leveling entire towns in a matter of hours. It's not just about a few degrees warmer or colder—it's about the entire system being thrown out of balance. This isn't just a problem for farmers or people who live in coastal areas; it's a problem for everyone, because we're all connected to the environment, whether we realize it or not.

Look at hurricanes for example. Even here in Atlanta, we're dealing with the threat of storms of increased intensity. The devastation wrought by Hurricane Helene in the Appalachians is heartbreaking, not the least of which because the region was so unprepared for that eventuality. Over the past few decades, there has been an increase in the intensity of hurricanes, especially in the Atlantic basin, likely linked to climate change. While the overall frequency of hurricanes has not shown a significant long-term trend, the proportion of high-intensity storms (Category 4 and 5) has increased since the 1980s. This trend is attributed to rising sea surface temperatures and increased atmospheric moisture, which provide more fuel for hurricanes, making them stronger and more destructive when they form [5][6]. The data shows that since the mid-20th century, there has been an unequivocal rise in the intensity and frequency of hurricanes in the North Atlantic, with models predicting that this will continue due to the ongoing effects of global warming. Higher sea surface temperatures contribute to stronger storms with more intense rainfall, higher wind speeds, and increased storm surges, exacerbating the overall impact of these events [7][8].

Growing Degree Days: A Crucial Measurement for Crop Production

Agricultural production is more complex than just planting seeds and harvesting crops. Each crop has a specific range of temperatures in which it can grow and produce optimally. One of the most important ways farmers and agricultural scientists measure this is through Growing Degree Days (GDDs). GDDs are a way to quantify heat accumulation over time, providing a metric to help predict when plants will reach key stages of development like germination, flowering, and maturity. It's like a biological calendar that uses temperature instead of days to mark the passage of time.

Each crop has a "base temperature," which is the minimum temperature required for its growth. For most crops, the base temperature is set between 5°C and 10°C (41°F to 50°F), but it varies depending on the species. Growing Degree Days are calculated by taking the average daily temperature and subtracting this base temperature. The accumulated GDDs over the growing season determine how quickly a crop moves through its life stages. This might sound like a technicality, but it's absolutely critical. If a crop accumulates GDDs too quickly due to higher-than-normal temperatures, it can reach maturity faster than expected. While that might sound like a good thing, it can lead to smaller yields, lower quality produce, and in some cases, complete crop failure.

Small changes in temperature variability can have a big impact on GDDs, which, in turn, has profound effects on crop production. For example, if the temperature is just a few degrees warmer than usual during critical growth periods, a crop may mature faster than anticipated, leading to premature flowering or fruiting. When this happens, the plant might not have enough time to develop strong root systems, resulting in weaker plants that are more susceptible to disease and pests. Conversely, if the temperature drops too low unexpectedly, it can slow growth or even cause damage to young plants not yet equipped to handle the stress. These fluctuations disrupt the delicate balance required for optimal crop growth. Imagine the chaos if all your Fourth of July watermelons matured on the

10th of June? It would be madness! Actually, watermelon can last for three to four weeks after harvest, but you get my point.

And the ripple effects of these disruptions extend far beyond the farm. Take wheat, for instance. A premature wheat harvest due to accelerated GDD accumulation can result in smaller kernels with lower protein content, impacting both the yield and quality of the flour produced. This, in turn, affects everything from bread to pasta to baked goods—raising prices across the entire supply chain. On a larger scale, significant shifts in GDDs can cause regional shifts in where crops are grown. As traditional growing zones become too warm or too cool, farmers may have to switch crops or abandon fields altogether, leading to localized food shortages and economic instability in agricultural communities.

Temperature variability can also affect when crops are harvested, throwing off the timing of supply chains that rely on precision. If a large portion of a crop is ready to harvest at once—due to a spike in GDDs—it can overwhelm processing facilities, causing delays and spoilage.

Case Study

In 2015, apple growers in the Pacific Northwest faced a significant disruption in their harvest due to extreme heat waves and erratic weather patterns. That year, the region experienced a severe drought and record-breaking temperatures, causing many crops to mature faster than usual. This accelerated growth led to a cascade of challenges for the apple industry, including an overwhelming supply of fruit ready to be harvested all at once.

As a result, many growers struggled to find enough labor and storage capacity, causing delays and an increase in spoilage. The quick ripening also resulted in quality issues such as sunburn (for the fruit, not the pickers; although to be fair, I don't know if anyone asked them) and reduced firmness (also for the fruit), making much of the crop less marketable. The economic impact was significant; some farms reported losing up to 50% of their Gala apple crop. Furthermore, the heat caused increased occurrence of disorders like bitter pit in apples, which affected storage and marketability even months after harvest. Even with the use of shade netting and overhead cooling, many orchards couldn't prevent damage to the fruit, leading to substantial losses for the season [9][10].

This situation underscored the vulnerability of agriculture to extreme weather events and highlighted the limitations of existing mitigation strategies, like shade netting, which were insufficient to protect apples from severe heat damage. The economic fallout went beyond the growers, affecting supply chains and prices, as processors and distributors had to deal with a glut of substandard fruit and uncertain storage conditions.

Overall, the 2015 apple crop in the Pacific Northwest serves as a stark example of how temperature variability and climate extremes can disrupt not just the timing and yield of a harvest, but also impact the entire supply chain from farm to consumer.

———————— ◆ ————————

Alternatively, if the crop is maturing slower than expected, processing plants and distributors may have to sit idle, waiting for the harvest to catch up. This unpredictability can wreak havoc on everything from local grocery store inventories to international commodity markets, ultimately resulting in price volatility and supply chain inefficiencies.

Simply put, even slight variations in temperature affect GDDs, and therefore, the growth and quality of crops. In a world where the climate is becoming more unpredictable, understanding and managing these small changes is critical. Farmers can adjust planting dates or use different crop varieties to better align with shifting GDD patterns, but those solutions come with their own challenges and costs. And as the climate continues to change, the margin for error narrows, making it more difficult for farmers to produce the stable, high-quality yields we've come to expect. So, when we talk about a "degree or two," it's not just about being a little warmer—it's about potentially rewriting the entire playbook for how, when, and where we grow our food. In other words, it's the entire foundation of our food system being shaken up like a snow globe… without the snow. Because of all the global warming. See what I did there?

Ecosystems: Not Just a Great Word to Use in Your Business Pitch

And it doesn't stop there. The ramifications of climate change ripple far beyond agriculture. Rising temperatures and changing rainfall patterns are also threatening water supplies, increasing the risk of wildfires, and accelerating the loss of biodiversity. Forests that have stood for centuries are being decimated by fires and pests they've never faced before. Oceans, which have absorbed much of the excess heat, are becoming warmer and more acidic, putting marine ecosystems under immense stress. Coral reefs—often called the "rainforests of the sea"—are bleaching and dying at unprecedented rates, wiping out vital fish habitats and jeopardizing the livelihoods of coastal communities. Glaciers and polar ice caps are melting at rates not seen in human history, contributing to rising sea levels that threaten to swallow coastal cities and entire island nations. And these changes aren't some distant future problem—they're happening right now, reshaping the world we thought we knew.

So, when we say "record-breaking heatwaves," we're not just talking about a few extra days at the beach. We're talking about a fundamental transformation of our environment that impacts everything from the food on your plate to the price of your morning latte. Climate change isn't just an environmental problem; it's an economic problem, a social problem, and, ultimately, a problem of human survival; my survival especially, if my wife doesn't get her coffee in the morning because it's too expensive. Don't worry, I won't get in trouble for that; I doubt she'll read this book. Seriously though, it's not just the farmers who are affected, but the entire web of life that supports us all. Every disrupted growing season, every failed harvest, every inch of coastline lost to the sea chips away at the stability of our interconnected world.

And that brings us back to agriculture, where the most immediate impacts are often felt first. Climate change is disrupting the entire agricultural system—from how crops are grown, to where they can be grown, to how much they yield, and ultimately, to what you pay at the grocery store. And if that doesn't catch your attention, maybe this will: the world's agriculture system is already struggling to keep up with a growing global population. Although global population growth is slower than projected just a few decades ago, it isn't slow enough to make a difference. Throwing climate change into the mix isn't just a nuisance; it's a game-changer, one that has the potential to undermine food security on a scale we've never seen before.

And the impacts are already being felt. According to the Intergovernmental Panel on Climate Change (IPCC), global agricultural productivity has already decreased by 21% since the 1960s due to climate-related factors like shifting rainfall patterns, extreme weather events, and rising temperatures[11]. That's one-fifth of the food we could have been producing—gone. If you think that's bad, hold on to your (organic, fair-trade) coffee, because the forecasts are even bleaker.

The Macro View: A Troubling Forecast

Let's start with some cold, hard numbers. The World Bank estimates that by 2050, global crop yields could decline by up to 25% due to climate change[12]. That's right—one in four crops could be wiped out. Staple crops like wheat and rice are expected to be hit the hardest, with the Food and Agriculture Organization (FAO) projecting yield losses of up to 30% in some regions[13]. If you live in a country that depends on imports for these staples, that means higher prices and potential food shortages. If you don't? Well, you'll feel it, too, because as supply tightens, prices go up everywhere.

For example, one study by the International Food Policy Research Institute (IFPRI) predicts that food prices could increase by as much as 70% globally by 2050 due to climate disruptions[14]. You thought the price of avocados was high now? Wait until a drought wipes out half the crop in California and a heatwave scorches the remainder in Mexico. You'll be trading your kid's Pokémon cards for guacamole on the black market. And let's not even get started on how this will affect coffee. There's already a projected 50% reduction in suitable land for coffee production by 2050[15], which means your morning cup of joe might become a luxury item.

It's not just crop yields that are at risk, though. Livestock and fisheries are also feeling the heat—literally. Higher temperatures are stressing cattle and reducing milk production. I don't like to work when it's hot either, so I don't blame them. Meanwhile, warmer ocean temperatures are causing fish populations to migrate to cooler waters, disrupting traditional fishing grounds. The domino effect is clear: less food, more competition for what's left, and rising prices that hit everyone, from big agricultural companies to consumers looking at their grocery bills in horror.

Economic Forecast: A Grim Outlook – Yippee!

All these disruptions add up to a significant hit on global economies. The World Bank estimates that the direct economic costs of climate change on agriculture could exceed $80 billion annually by 2050[16]. And that's just for the agricultural sector itself. If you factor in the ripple effects—such as increased healthcare costs due to malnutrition, lost workdays from heat stress, and social unrest from food shortages—the numbers climb even higher.

In low-income countries, where a large percentage of the population depends on agriculture for both income and sustenance, the situation is even more dire. According to the FAO, smallholder farmers in Africa and Asia could see their incomes drop by up to 70% as climate change reduces crop yields and disrupts local markets[17][18]. For these communities, it's not just about fewer earnings; it's about survival. When your entire income is tied to what you can grow (and when you can grow it), and suddenly your farm is producing half of what it used to, you're faced with impossible choices—cut back on food, sell off livestock, or abandon farming altogether.

But this isn't just a problem for developing countries. In the United States, a recent study by the USDA projected that agricultural output could decline by 10% to 20% by 2050, depending on the severity of climate impacts[19]. That's a potential loss of hundreds of billions of dollars to the economy—money that affects not just farmers, but the entire supply chain, from food processors to retailers. And when food prices spike, they don't just pinch your wallet— they pinch the broader economy. Higher food prices reduce disposable income, which in turn lowers demand for non-food goods and services, slowing economic growth. In other words, we all pay the price.

Bringing it Home: From Global Crisis to Your Shopping Cart

If the phrase "global agricultural productivity decline" makes your eyes glaze over, you're not alone. Mine did too, and I was the one typing it. So, let's bring it home. Imagine walking into your favorite grocery store and noticing that your usual $3.99 pint of strawberries is now $7.99. It's not some new reverse marketing trend, unfortunately— just the new normal. The thing is, this isn't just a story of higher prices. It's a story of inequity. As food becomes more expensive, those with lower incomes will feel the squeeze hardest, leading to higher rates of food insecurity even in wealthy countries. Food banks, already struggling to meet demand, could see even longer lines. Suddenly, your choice of breakfast cereal isn't between Frosted Flakes and Cheerios; it's between a meal or none at all for many families.

And let's not forget about food deserts—urban and rural areas where access to affordable, nutritious food is already severely limited. These are the neighborhoods where grocery stores are few and far between, and fast-food chains dominate. With climate change threatening to increase food prices and decrease availability, these food deserts could turn into full-fledged food wastelands. Fresh produce, already a rarity in these areas, may become a luxury item, further deepening health disparities. In communities where diet-related diseases like diabetes and hypertension are already prevalent, a lack of healthy food options could have devastating consequences. The issue is systemic: as prices go up, more stores might choose to stock fewer fresh products, leading to even greater reliance on processed, less nutritious options.

Expanding on the potential economic impact of diet-related diseases like diabetes and hypertension on the healthcare system, it's clear that the costs are staggering and could worsen with increasing food insecurity due to climate change. In the United States alone, diabetes currently costs the healthcare system an estimated $412.9 billion annually, with $306.6 billion attributed to direct medical costs and an additional $106.3 billion in indirect costs such as lost productivity and unemployment from chronic disability[20]. Similarly, cardiovascular diseases, including hypertension, cost the healthcare system $254 billion annually and result in $168 billion in lost productivity[21].

Poor diet choices, which are a direct consequence of limited access to healthy foods, are responsible for around 20% of U.S. healthcare costs related to heart disease, stroke, and type 2 diabetes, contributing an additional $50 billion each year[22].

As climate change disrupts food supply chains and increases the cost of fresh produce, food deserts are likely to expand, further limiting access to nutritious options. This can exacerbate existing health disparities and inflate healthcare costs even more.

If agricultural output continues to decline and food prices increase, lower-income communities—already vulnerable to diet-related diseases—could face even more significant health challenges, putting further strain on healthcare systems and public health budgets. These economic pressures will not only impact healthcare spending but could also influence national productivity and economic stability as a whole.

It's not just staple food prices either. Take chocolate, for example. Rising temperatures and erratic rainfall are already threatening cacao production in West Africa, which supplies about 70% of the world's cocoa. Scientists project that by 2050, a large portion of the land currently used for cacao cultivation will no longer be suitable. That's bad news if you're a chocolate lover—and even worse if you're a chocolatier. Sorry, Willy Wonka. Expect chocolate bars to get smaller, more expensive, and less available. A future where a single, palm-sized piece of dark chocolate costs $20 may seem far-fetched, but if the trends continue, it might become a reality.

To bring it all together, we're looking at an estimated $495 billion in additional annual cost to American households by 2050 just on food. When accounting for the impact of agricultural increases on other sectors like healthcare, logistics, transportation, energy, retail, hospitality, finance and insurance, estimates north of $1 trillion annually are well within reason. These net additional economic costs represent not just a financial burden, but also a profound shift in global economic stability, requiring significant investment and adaptation efforts to mitigate the worst outcomes. And these numbers are just for the United States. Calculating the total global impact scared me too much to try.

And it's not just about rising prices or economic statistics—these disruptions could result in widespread job losses in agriculture-dependent communities, increased strain on public services, and reduced quality of life for millions of people globally.

Stakeholder Analysis: Who's Impacted and Why You Should Care

When agriculture suffers, it's not just farmers who lose out—it's everyone. Let's look at the key stakeholders and how they're impacted by this complex web of climate disruptions:

- *Smallholder Farmers*: Already operating on razor-thin margins, these farmers are hit hardest by climate change. As yields decline, costs rise, and competition for resources intensifies, many are being forced to abandon farming entirely. This, in turn, destabilizes rural communities, leading to a cycle of poverty and food insecurity. I'll admit, I'm a little biased in favor of this group. They have historically been excluded from participating in the market at the same level as their larger counterparts. Limited access to education, training, technology, finance and markets has meant they typically have been at the mercy of middlemen who cut deep into the profits of what these farmers keep. With the deck already stacked against them, adding the negative impacts of climate change on top of it only exacerbates the inequity of the situation.
- *Large Agricultural Companies*: You might think that big corporations like Monsanto or Cargill can weather the storm, but they're also highly vulnerable. Crop failures and changing growing conditions force these companies to rethink their supply chains, invest in new technologies, and hedge against greater financial risks. In the long run, climate change threatens their profitability and even their ability to function. And love them or hate them, they inarguably form an integral part of ensuring we all get to eat.
- Governments: Countries that rely on agriculture for a significant portion of their GDP—think India, Brazil, and many African nations—face the double threat of economic losses and social instability. When food prices spike, people protest. And when people protest, governments face pressure to act, often

leading to politically destabilizing measures like price controls or subsidies that strain national budgets. But the policy responses don't stop there. When food security becomes a national issue, governments often implement export bans or quotas to protect domestic supply, as we've seen in countries like India, which periodically restricts rice and wheat exports. These measures are intended to stabilize local markets, but they can have far-reaching impacts on global food prices, further driving up costs for import-dependent nations and creating a vicious cycle of food insecurity.

- On the flip side, import-reliant countries may respond with tariffs or subsidies on imported goods to support local agriculture and reduce dependence on volatile global markets. While these policies aim to build food self-sufficiency, they can distort market prices and make it harder for consumers to afford basic necessities. And in a world where agricultural outputs are declining due to climate change, such policies can inadvertently lead to global supply chain disruptions, reducing availability and pushing prices even higher.

- Governments may also turn to heavier regulation and oversight of food production and distribution to maintain stability, which can impose additional compliance costs on producers. This often drives smaller farms out of business, consolidating power in the hands of large agribusinesses and further reducing competition. Ultimately, food security concerns can lead to a patchwork of conflicting policies—like subsidies in one country and tariffs in another—that isolate markets, reduce efficiency, and create additional economic burdens for both producers and consumers. And as each country tries to shield its citizens from the impacts of rising food prices, the unintended consequences often spill over across borders, intensifying global food shortages and making it harder to achieve coordinated international solutions.

- *Consumers*: That's you. It might be tempting to think that this is a problem for far-off places or someone else's dinner table. But when your grocery bill doubles, or your favorite foods become harder to find, it's your lifestyle that changes. We've focused very heavily on food prices and availability as impacted by changes to the global agriculture sector, but there are two other big parts of agriculture that directly affect consumers: fuel and fiber.

Fuel: The Hidden Cost of Agricultural Disruption

- Agriculture and fuel are deeply intertwined, and disruptions in one can have profound effects on the other. For starters, biofuels—such as ethanol and biodiesel—are major agricultural products derived from crops like corn, sugarcane, and soybeans. The global biofuel industry is heavily influenced by the availability and price of these crops. So, when climate change causes yields to drop or prices to spike, the cost of producing biofuels rises as well, leading to a cascading effect on energy prices. In the United States, for example, approximately 40% of the corn crop is used to produce ethanol. A reduction in corn production doesn't just mean Orville Redenbacher has to dig a little deeper to fill those popcorn bags; it also means higher prices at the gas pump.

- But it's not just about biofuels. The agricultural sector is also one of the largest consumers of fossil fuels. Tractors, irrigation systems, transportation of goods—nearly every step in the agricultural supply chain requires energy. As crop yields decline and prices rise, the energy costs associated with producing, processing, and distributing agricultural products will only increase. This creates a feedback loop: higher fuel prices make agricultural production more expensive, which further drives up food prices. Meanwhile, as farmers and food processors pay more for energy, they pass those costs on to consumers, which means you're not just paying more for food—you're paying more at the gas station too. This dual impact can contribute to inflationary pressures throughout the economy, squeezing household budgets even further.

Fiber: Beyond Food—The Textile Impact

- Let's not forget about fiber. Cotton, the fabric of our lives (everyone reading this is old enough to remember that, right?), one of the most widely grown agricultural commodities in the world, is used to produce everything from your favorite pair of jeans to the sheets on your bed. Just like food crops, cotton is highly sensitive to changes in temperature and water availability. Extreme heat and irregular rainfall patterns can significantly reduce cotton yields or degrade the quality of the fiber, resulting in less supply and, consequently, higher prices for consumers.

- In fact, a study by the International Cotton Advisory Committee (ICAC) suggests that if current climate trends continue, cotton production could decline by as much as 10% by 2050, driving up global cotton prices by 50% or more. That may not sound like much in isolation but consider this: the cost of raw materials makes up a substantial portion of the overall price of clothing. A significant rise in cotton prices can make everything from T-shirts to high-end fashion more expensive. As clothing manufacturers try to absorb these costs, we're likely to see either lower-quality garments flooding the market or sharp increases in clothing prices. And that's not just a first-world problem—textile production is a major source of employment in countries like India, Bangladesh, and Vietnam. Reduced cotton availability and higher prices could lead to factory closures, layoffs, and a surge in poverty in these regions, further straining global social and economic stability.

- But it's not just cotton. Agriculture is also the source of many other natural fibers like wool, flax (linen), and hemp. Each of these fibers is sensitive to climate fluctuations in different ways. For example, warmer temperatures can cause sheep to produce less wool, and droughts can reduce flax and hemp yields. As a result, we might see more consumers turning to synthetic fibers like polyester and nylon. However, increased reliance on synthetic materials has its own set of environmental and economic drawbacks, including greater dependency on fossil fuels for production and a higher environmental footprint due to microplastic pollution. Also, what will the sheep do for work? Think of the sheep, man!

The Broader Consumer Impact

The combination of higher fuel and fiber costs creates a multi-layered problem for consumers. It's not just that your morning cereal costs more—now your commute to work is pricier, and your budget for new clothes is stretched thin. These disruptions in food, fuel, and fiber markets are not isolated; they are interconnected threads in the fabric of our global economy. When one thread frays, the entire system becomes more fragile, increasing the risk of economic instability and social unrest.

In other words, the consequences of agricultural disruptions don't just show up in your grocery bill—they're embedded in the price of everything you consume. From the gas in your car to the clothes in your closet, the ripple effects of a less productive and more volatile agricultural system are felt across every aspect of daily life. This is why understanding the broader implications of climate change on agriculture is crucial. It's not just about protecting farms—it's about maintaining the stability and affordability of the products that underpin our way of life.

Wrapping Up a Really Uplifting Chapter

That was a lot of information and not much of it is good news. By now, it should be clear that climate change isn't just a problem for distant fields and faceless farmers. It's a problem for your kitchen table, your closet, and your community. Whether it's skyrocketing food prices, shrinking cotton supplies, or higher gas bills, the disruptions to agriculture will be felt in every aspect of daily life. The stakes are high, and the path forward is fraught with challenges. As we've seen, the ripple effects extend far beyond farmers' fields, threatening global supply chains, economic stability, and even geopolitical security.

But we're not helpless in the face of these changes. In the next chapter, we'll take a closer look at what's being done—and what more can be done—to address this terrifying potential future. We'll explore the policies, programs, and technologies currently in use to build a more resilient agricultural system and tackle climate change head-on. We'll also examine their limitations and the gaps that still need to be filled. Because while the problems are daunting, they are not insurmountable. And knowing what we're up against is the first step toward building a system that's sustainable not just for today, but for generations to come.

4
State of (in)Action

If the previous chapters have left you feeling a little on edge, don't worry—you're not alone. At this point, you're probably wondering: "Surely, the people in charge have a plan, right?" Well, yes... and no. First, you assume there are people in charge...you're an optimist, I like that. Second, welcome to the murky, bureaucratic soup of current climate policies and programs. The good news? There are plenty of efforts underway to tackle climate change and make agriculture more sustainable. The bad news? Many of them are like a Band-Aid on a bullet wound—well-intentioned but woefully inadequate.

Current Policies and Programs: An Overview of the Global Patchwork

Let's start by taking a whirlwind tour around the world. Almost every country has some sort of policy or initiative aimed at combating climate change. However, when you peel back the glossy press releases, you quickly see that many of these efforts lack the teeth to bite into the problem. And, just like the '08 Detroit Lions, they often fail to coordinate with each other leading to lackluster results.

The Paris Agreement: Ah, the darling of international climate diplomacy. *Le Petite Promesse*, as everyone calls it. Well, I don't think anyone else calls it that, but it's a pretty good nickname and I'm hoping it will catch on. Signed by 196 countries, it aims to keep global warming below 2°C. Sounds great, right? But the agreement is more like a New Year's resolution: everyone nods enthusiastically at the beginning, and then promptly forgets about it by February. It's non-binding and relies on countries voluntarily setting their own emissions targets. This has led to what we'll generously call a "diverse" set of commitments, with some countries aiming for carbon neutrality by 2050, while others are apparently content to hit that mark sometime around the next ice age.

And look, everybody likes to dump on the Paris Agreement because it's easy and being cynical can be fun. But, despite its non-binding nature and the varied levels of commitment from participating countries, the Paris Agreement does have several promising aspects that are already making an impact:

Global Participation and Ambition: The most significant win of the Paris Agreement is the sheer number of countries that have signed on—196 to be exact. While commitments may vary, this is the first time virtually the entire world has agreed on the need to take action on climate change. The global nature of the agreement has spurred greater international cooperation and created a framework where countries are at least discussing emissions reductions, even if implementation is uneven. For example, the European Union and several individual countries have implemented ambitious plans to achieve carbon neutrality by 2050, with the EU's European Green Deal setting a legally binding target of net-zero emissions by that date.

Nationally Determined Contributions: One of the key features of the Paris Agreement is that it allows countries to set their own climate action goals, known as Nationally Determined Contributions (NDCs). While this flexibility has led to varying levels of ambition, it also means that countries can tailor their climate actions to their specific circumstances. Encouragingly, many countries have begun updating and enhancing their NDCs, with countries like China, India, and South Korea committing to more aggressive emissions reductions and renewable energy targets in recent years.

Long-Term Strategy Development: The agreement encourages countries to develop long-term low greenhouse gas emission development strategies (LT-LEDS), which focus on decarbonizing economies by mid-century. Countries like Germany, France, and Canada have already created detailed plans outlining how they will transition to carbon-neutral economies. These strategies focus on areas such as transitioning to renewable energy, enhancing energy efficiency, and investing in sustainable infrastructure.

Climate Finance: The Paris Agreement has put a spotlight on the importance of financing climate action, especially for developing countries. Wealthier nations committed to mobilizing $100 billion annually by 2020 to help lower-income countries adapt to climate impacts and transition to cleaner energy. And just like me and this book's publishing deadline, they hit their target right on time…in 2022. But late is better than never which is honestly what most people in the climate world expected (reference cynicism being fun).

Global Stocktake: Every five years, the Paris Agreement calls for a global stocktake—a comprehensive assessment of how well countries are meeting their climate goals and what more needs to be done. This stocktake allows countries to recalibrate their efforts and encourages them to increase their ambition over time. The first official global stocktake was scheduled for 2023, and early signs indicated that it would put additional pressure on countries to step up their climate commitments and actions. Well, that didn't work out quite like everyone had hoped.

The first-ever Global Stocktake, which concluded in 2023 at COP28, revealed a sobering reality: the world is not on track to meet the long-term goals of the Paris Agreement. The stocktake process highlighted a significant gap between current climate action and the commitments necessary to limit global warming to 1.5°C. It showed that, despite the near-universal adoption of the Paris Agreement, emissions continue to rise, and the world remains on a trajectory toward a temperature increase of approximately 2.7°C by the end of the century.

The stocktake process involved reviewing data from national climate plans, scientific reports, and stakeholder inputs. It called for more urgent and coordinated actions to close the gap in emission reductions, particularly with respect to strengthening national climate commitments, or NDCs, as mentioned earlier. While the report painted a grim picture of current progress, it also pointed to advancements in certain areas, such as renewable energy and climate finance.

Non-State Actors and Private Sector Engagement: Another promising aspect of the Paris Agreement is how it has galvanized action from non-state actors, including cities, corporations, and civil society organizations. Major companies have pledged to achieve net-zero emissions, and cities like New York and Paris are rolling out ambitious local climate plans. These actors are increasingly seen as critical drivers of climate action, helping to fill the gap left by slower-moving national policies. However, as we'll examine later, pledges and plans do not always equate to honest action and so other measures must be taken to ensure not just compliance, but the credibility of the movement.

In short, while the Paris Agreement isn't perfect and has its fair share of shortcomings, its global participation, growing ambition from NDCs, focus on long-term strategies, and mobilization of climate finance and private sector engagement are promising aspects that are helping push the world toward a more sustainable future.

The EU's Common Agricultural Policy (CAP): Europe's Common Agricultural Policy (CAP) is a perfect example of a well-intentioned initiative that often misses the mark. The CAP was originally designed to support farmers, ensure food security, and promote sustainable agricultural practices across the EU. In theory, this sounds like a win for both the environment and small farmers. However, in practice, it has faced significant criticism for disproportionately benefiting large-scale industrial farms at the expense of small/family farms and truly sustainable farming.

Here's how it works: the CAP distributes subsidies to farmers based on the amount of land they cultivate, rather than on the environmental benefits they provide or the sustainability of their practices. This incentivizes large landowners to dominate the system, receiving substantial payments simply because they control more acreage. For instance, 80% of CAP payments go to just 20% of the largest farms, many of which engage in intensive, high-input farming that contributes to soil degradation, biodiversity loss, and increased carbon emissions.

Instead of promoting the environmental goals it was intended to foster, the CAP has, in many cases, driven the expansion of monocultures and industrial-scale farming practices that deplete natural resources and damage ecosystems. It's like hopping on TikTok to brag about being committed to sustainable living from your private jet because, you know, you'll "offset the emissions" later.

We can all relate to that, am I right?

In recent years, the EU has tried to introduce more environmental reforms to the CAP, including requirements for "greening measures" like crop rotation and preserving permanent grasslands. But these reforms have often been criticized as weak or easily circumvented. For example, farmers can technically meet the greening criteria by planting different varieties of the same crop or by minimally rotating crops, which doesn't address the underlying issue of soil depletion or biodiversity loss.

As a result, small farmers—who are often better positioned to adopt truly sustainable practices—are being squeezed out, while larger industrial farms, which contribute more to environmental degradation, are reaping the benefits of the subsidy system. This creates a paradox where policies meant to promote sustainability are inadvertently fueling the very practices driving us closer to environmental collapse.

It's as if the CAP is an elaborate diet plan that promises a healthier tomorrow but allows you to gorge on cake today, with the vague promise that you'll burn off those calories eventually.

India's National Action Plan on Climate Change (NAPCC): India's strategy includes the National Mission for Sustainable Agriculture, which aims to support climate-resilient farming. But with 70% of the country's population dependent on agriculture, the mission is more like a drop in a rapidly drying bucket. Many farmers are unaware of the programs, and those who do know find the application processes as complicated as filing taxes while blindfolded. Several individual states have started their own initiatives to tackle sustainable agriculture. The state of Telangana, for example, announced a program in 2022 to convert a large area of rice paddies to oil palm cultivation. On the face of it, that sounds terrible, mostly because oil palm has such a (often well deserved) bad reputation in the environmental sector. But India is a net exporter of rice and a big importer of palm oil. That demand for palm oil helps drive deforestation in other parts of the world like Indonesia and Malaysia. Reduction in transportation and logistics impact means a smaller scope 3 carbon footprint, the elimination of that rice cultivation eliminates significant methane emissions and the trees themselves sequester carbon for as long as the trees are productive. By creating a domestic supply of palm oil from land already cultivating a surplus of one crop, the net benefits far outweigh any negatives that come from replacing one monoculture with another.

The U.S. Farm Bill: The U.S. Farm Bill is a massive piece of legislation that, among other things (80% goes to the Supplemental Nutrition Assistance Program-SNAP), funds conservation programs like the Environmental Quality Incentives Program (EQIP) to help farmers implement sustainable practices. But with its tangled web of requirements and preferences for large agricultural operations, many small farmers are left scratching their heads, wondering if it's worth the hassle. Average acceptance rates are less than 30% nationally. The bill also tends to prioritize staple crops like corn and soybeans— making it easier to grow more of what's already contributing to climate issues and harder to switch to more sustainable crops.

The Inflation Reduction Act (IRA), passed in 2022, includes significant provisions aimed at addressing the sustainability issues embedded in U.S. agriculture, which have often been exacerbated by policies like the U.S. Farm Bill's focus on staple crops like corn and soybeans. The IRA allocates $20 billion to strengthen agricultural conservation programs that aim to promote more sustainable farming practices and mitigate the effects of climate change. Specifically:

Funding for Conservation Programs: The IRA significantly boosts funding for existing conservation programs like the Environmental Quality Incentives Program (EQIP), the Conservation Stewardship Program (CSP), and the Agricultural Conservation Easement Program (ACEP). These programs provide financial and technical support to farmers looking to adopt sustainable practices, such as reducing greenhouse gas emissions, improving water quality, and preserving biodiversity. By increasing funding, the IRA makes these programs more accessible to small and medium-sized farmers who may have previously found them out of reach due to bureaucratic hurdles or limited availability.

Climate-Smart Agriculture: The IRA also focuses on encouraging climate-smart agricultural practices by allocating resources specifically for carbon sequestration projects, soil health initiatives, and reducing methane emissions from livestock. This is a step toward helping farmers transition to more sustainable crops and practices, reducing their reliance on high-emission staple crops like corn and soybeans, which are heavily subsidized by the Farm Bill.

Support for Diverse and Small-Scale Farms: One of the IRA's key improvements over previous legislation is that it addresses some of the disparities in funding access. Historically, large agricultural operations have had easier access to government funding due to their size and resources. The IRA provides more tailored support for small-scale farms, aiming to lower the barriers for them to adopt sustainable practices, such as organic farming, agroforestry, and regenerative agriculture.

Carbon Sequestration and Methane Reduction: The

IRA allocates funding to initiatives that aim to promote carbon sequestration—the process of capturing and storing atmospheric carbon dioxide in soils, trees, and other vegetation—through improved soil management techniques. It also targets reductions in methane emissions, a potent greenhouse gas, particularly from livestock operations. This creates incentives for farmers to shift towards more climate-friendly practices without solely relying on expanding production of staple crops like corn and soybeans, which have been criticized for their environmental impact.

Addressing Climate Resilience: With the increasing impact of climate change on agriculture, the IRA provides funding to help farmers become more resilient to climate impacts like droughts, floods, and extreme weather events. This is particularly beneficial for smaller farmers who may not have the capital to invest in climate adaptation technologies without government support.

In short, the Inflation Reduction Act is a substantial effort to redirect some of the U.S. agricultural system's focus from large-scale, industrial farming toward more sustainable practices. While the U.S. Farm Bill still prioritizes staple crops and often leaves small farmers grappling with complex requirements, the IRA's additional funding for conservation and sustainability initiatives offers hope that more farmers—especially smaller, more diverse operations—will have access to the resources they need to contribute to climate action.

However, the real challenge will be ensuring that these funds are distributed effectively and equitably, especially to those smaller-scale farmers who may still face barriers in navigating the complexities of federal programs. As of the writing of this book, much of the funds for the IRA have yet to be disbursed or even allocated. Even mechanisms for accessing the funds are yet to be finalized for American farmers. So, the level of impact will necessarily depend on the actual accessibility of the funds by the people who can actually put it to best use.

That's a lot of different policy efforts and really, it's just scratching the surface. Around the world, you'll find other initiatives like the Great Green Wall in Africa, which aims to combat desertification by planting trees (a noble idea, though one plagued by inconsistent implementation), and China's Grain-for-Green program, which incentivizes farmers to switch from crop cultivation to forestation in erosion-prone areas (another well-meaning effort that's seen mixed results). The point of this long list is that there is not a lack of effort in tackling the problem, but there is a lack of consistency, coordination and cooperation.

At this point, it's pretty clear that while there are no shortage of policies and programs, they're often like trying to bail water out of a sinking ship with a teaspoon. On one hand, you've got the Paris Agreement, providing a global platform for countries to make commitments to reduce emissions and support climate finance. On the other, you've got fragmented national policies like the CAP, the Farm Bill, and initiatives like India's National Action Plan on Climate Change that are rife with inefficiencies, misaligned incentives, and questionable results.

What ties all of these together is that they represent an earnest but insufficient attempt to tackle an overwhelming problem. While some progress is being made—countries are making stronger commitments, private sector involvement is ramping up, and significant funding is finally being unlocked—there's still a gap between what's being done and what needs to be done. To paraphrase that famous line from Jaws: "We're gonna need a bigger boat."

Unfortunately, the same barriers that have always existed—bureaucratic red tape, misaligned incentives, and the prioritization of short-term economic gains over long-term environmental health—continue to stand in the way of effective, large-scale climate action. The tools are there; what's missing is the political will, the coordination, and the systems to make it all work together.

In the second half of this chapter, we'll dive into some of the technological innovations that have the potential to transform agriculture and help mitigate climate change, from precision farming to drought-resistant crops. But, spoiler alert: like the policies we've just explored, they too come with their own set of limitations and challenges.

Let's keep going and see how these tools can—or can't—fit into the bigger picture of tackling climate change.

Technological Innovations and Limitations: Can Science Save Us?

Now, let's turn our attention to the shiny toys: technological innovations. If policy is the dull butter knife in this fight, technology is supposed to be the chef's knife—precise, effective, and capable of slicing through the toughest problems. Great tech can solve so many problems, it can even solve problems you didn't even know you had. Being the CEO of a tech company, I can say that with great confidence and no sarcasm whatsoever. Tech in the agriculture and, to a lesser extent, environmental space, has been hyped to solve many of the problems plaguing the sector. But even the best tools have limitations.

Drought-Resistant Crops: Scientists are working hard to develop drought-resistant crops that can survive in harsher conditions. Sounds like a miracle, right? Well, yes and no. While these crops have shown promise, they often require specific conditions to thrive. Moreover, the genetics that make them drought-resistant can sometimes reduce their resistance to pests or lower their nutritional value. So, you might end up with a crop that can grow in a desert... but is still destroyed by a single locust.

Precision Agriculture: Using drones, satellites, and AI, precision agriculture aims to optimize every drop of water and every gram of fertilizer. Farmers can analyze soil health in real-time and make data-driven decisions. It's like having the Iron Man suit for farming! The problem? It's prohibitively expensive and requires tech-savviness that many farmers—particularly older or smaller-scale ones—don't have. Imagine handing your grandparents the latest iPhone and asking them to build a rocket ship. Yeah, it's kind of like that. One of the other major problems with precision farming is despite the name, the solutions it recommends are still rather generic. Sure, within a field you can get variable input rate recommendations, but they are based on data that is significantly less granular and unique to that specific field than the name would suggest. The real precision in precision agriculture lies in the application of inputs. Computer driven hardware points on good old-fashioned iron can put exactly the amount of fertilizer/herbicide/pesticide/fairy dust that has been prescribed exactly where it is supposed to be applied. The problem is in getting the doctor to write the correct prescription.

Internet of Things (IoT) and Smart Irrigation Systems: IoT sensors can measure soil moisture levels and automatically adjust irrigation to minimize water use. Great! But if you're a smallholder farmer in Kenya or Vietnam, affording these systems is a pipe dream. Even in wealthier countries, the upfront costs and maintenance expenses can be a major barrier, limiting their adoption to only the wealthiest and largest farms. Also, maintaining sensitive hardware in the field sucks. I say that from experience. I've lost sensors to tractors, combines, rats, wild boar and alligators. Yes, you heard me, alligators.

Side Story: I once missed a flight home from a field visit to a customer in south Florida because of those scaly dwarf dinosaurs. It was early on the final morning of the visit, and I needed to go replace the last of the malfunctioning sensors. Dawn hadn't yet broken but if I hurried, I could get the sensor swapped and make my flight back to Atlanta. So, I parked along the access road and started walking out through the sugarcane to find the broken sensor. If you've never been in mature sugarcane before, imagine much taller, thicker and more densely planted corn stalks that give you about 5 feet of visibility in broad daylight and it'll give you an idea. About 40 feet into the row, still dark, I hear a rustling in the cane a few yards away. Having seen a dozen fun sized gators the previous day, my mind begins imagining how tasty I would be for breakfast. Long story short, the sensor didn't get replaced until well after the sun came up and I had to rebook my flight for later in the evening. But I was able to keep all my fingers and toes so all's well that ends well.

Vertical Farming and Controlled Environment Agriculture (CEA): Growing food in stacked layers within controlled environments is another promising innovation, reducing water use by up to 90% and eliminating the need for pesticides. But scalability is the Achilles' heel here. Building and maintaining vertical farms is incredibly expensive, and they're currently limited to high-value crops like herbs, lettuce, microgreens and, well, herb (if you know what I mean). Want to grow wheat or rice this way? Good luck—you'll need a skyscraper-sized farm and a billionaire's budget.

One of the great things about CEA, though, is its interoperability with other technological advances. When you control every environmental variable and can put sensors just about anywhere, you can maintain complete control over every application at an extremely precise level. This means totally optimized input efficiency and a greater ability to tap into renewable energy sources for these types of applications. The environmental downside is that you miss out on one big renewable energy source, natural UV from the sun, which apparently is important for plants to grow.

Carbon Sequestration and Soil Health: Agricultural soils are a massive carbon sink, and technologies aimed at enhancing soil carbon sequestration could play a significant role in mitigating climate change. Techniques like regenerative agriculture, no-till farming, and the use of biochar are designed to capture and store more carbon in soils, reducing the amount of CO_2 in the atmosphere. Biochar, for instance, is a charcoal-like substance produced by heating organic matter in the absence of oxygen. When applied to soils, it not only improves soil fertility but also sequesters carbon for centuries. Biochar also has a ton of other potential uses that would likewise sequester carbon for hundreds of years including its use in construction materials, municipal waste treatment, water filtration, and even in a highly refined form as graphene for use in batteries.

In addition to soil management, carbon capture and storage (CCS) technologies are being explored to directly capture CO_2 emissions from industrial sources, such as power plants, and store them underground. While CCS has the potential to remove large amounts of CO_2 from the atmosphere, the technology is still expensive, energy-intensive, and not yet scalable at the levels needed to make a major dent in global emissions.

Methane Reduction in Livestock: Methane, a potent GHG, is a major byproduct of livestock farming, particularly from enteric fermentation (cow burps) and manure management. Several new technologies and feed additives are being developed to reduce methane emissions from cattle. For instance, seaweed-based feed additives have shown potential in reducing methane emissions from ruminants by up to 80%. Another example is methane digesters, which capture methane from manure and convert it into biogas, a renewable source of energy.

While these innovations hold great promise, they are not without challenges. The scalability of feed additives for global livestock herds, for example, remains uncertain, and methane digesters require significant capital investment and infrastructure, limiting their use to larger farming operations.

Greenhouse Gas Monitoring, Reporting, and Verification (MRV): Accurate measurement of GHG emissions is critical for any climate mitigation effort. Advanced MRV systems, often powered by AI and remote sensing technologies, are being deployed to track emissions across sectors more accurately. These technologies are crucial for carbon credit markets, where reliable data on emission reductions and sequestration is essential for trading carbon offsets. AI-driven systems can analyze satellite images, IoT sensor data, and other sources to provide real-time reports on GHG emissions.

However, the challenge with MRV systems is ensuring data transparency and accountability. As the carbon market grows, the potential for fraud or manipulation in carbon offset claims becomes a concern. Ensuring these systems are robust and widely adopted is a crucial next step.

Renewable Energy and Electrification of Agriculture: The shift to renewable energy—from solar and wind power to biofuels—also plays a crucial role in reducing agriculture's carbon footprint. Farmers can adopt solar-powered irrigation, electric tractors, and other clean technologies to reduce reliance on fossil fuels. Countries like India are promoting the adoption of solar pumps to replace diesel-powered irrigation systems, significantly cutting down GHG emissions while providing a more reliable energy source for farmers. In the United States, grants and tax incentives offer ways for farmers to recoup their capital expenditure for these improvements sometimes in as little as seven months. But a major limiting factor is program awareness as well as a lack of reputable firms dealing in systems, installation and maintenance. While many great companies exist that offer these services, there are also a large number of fly-by-night operations with limited oversight, either formal or informal.

Direct Air Capture (DAC): DAC is one of the more ambitious and rapidly advancing climate technologies designed to mitigate the buildup of greenhouse gases in the atmosphere. Unlike traditional carbon capture methods, which target emissions from specific sources like power plants, DAC involves capturing CO_2 directly from the ambient air. Using large fans and chemical processes, DAC systems pull air into facilities where the CO_2 is extracted and either stored underground in geological formations or repurposed for products like synthetic fuels, concrete, or plastics. It's like giant artificial trees that actually do something other than gather dust in the corner of our living room.

The appeal of DAC lies in its potential to achieve negative emissions—removing more CO_2 from the atmosphere than is being emitted—making it a critical tool in scenarios where decarbonizing certain sectors, like aviation or heavy industry, is extremely difficult. Companies like Climeworks and Carbon Engineering are leading the way, with operational DAC plants already capturing thousands of tons of CO_2 annually. However, scaling up remains a significant challenge. DAC is energy-intensive and currently expensive, with estimates ranging from $100 to $600 per ton of CO_2 removed. To reach the necessary scale to make a significant climate impact, massive investments and technological improvements are needed to lower costs and enhance efficiency.

While DAC offers exciting possibilities for carbon removal, it's crucial to recognize that it is not a substitute for reducing emissions at the source. Instead, it should be viewed as part of a broader portfolio of climate solutions, ideally working in conjunction with renewable energy, reforestation, and emissions reductions across all sectors.

Enhanced Rock Weathering (ERW): This is an innovative geoengineering technique that seeks to accelerate the natural process of rock weathering to capture and sequester atmospheric carbon dioxide (CO_2). In nature, rocks like basalt naturally absorb CO_2 through chemical reactions as they break down over time, eventually locking away carbon in stable mineral forms. ERW aims to speed up this process by crushing silicate rocks into fine particles and spreading them over agricultural land or coastal environments. The fine particles increase the surface area for chemical reactions, allowing them to capture more CO_2 from the atmosphere much faster than in their natural state.

One of the key benefits of ERW is that it can be integrated into existing agricultural practices. The finely ground rock dust can be applied to soils as a supplement to improve soil health while also capturing carbon. As the minerals dissolve, they neutralize soil acidity, enhancing nutrient availability and potentially increasing crop yields. Additionally, ERW could help mitigate ocean acidification by increasing the alkalinity of runoff waters, providing a buffer against rising carbon levels in the marine environment.

While the potential for ERW is promising, there are significant challenges. The method requires large amounts of rock material, energy-intensive grinding, and extensive transportation and distribution to have a measurable impact on global carbon levels. Moreover, the actual rate at which CO_2 is captured and sequestered depends on various factors like climate, soil conditions, and the type of rock used. Despite these hurdles, research continues to explore ERW as a scalable solution for carbon removal, particularly in combination with other carbon capture and sequestration strategies.

This list of technologies is by no means exhaustive and within each category mentioned here, entire books could be written on the various subcomponents. But in summary, while technological advances offer exciting possibilities, they are not a panacea. Many of these innovations are still in their infancy and come with a host of challenges related to cost, accessibility, and scalability. And without supportive policies and financing, they're unlikely to reach the farmers who need them most which means their potential impact is limited at best.

Finance Mechanisms: The Financial Labyrinth Farmers Face

Let's take a little detour through the bewildering maze of financial incentives. Imagine a day in the life of a farmer trying to navigate these programs.

Our hypothetical farmer, let's call him Mr. Patel, starts his morning with a strong cup of tea. He's heard about carbon markets where he could potentially sell "carbon credits" by adopting sustainable practices. So, he picks up the phone and calls his local agricultural extension office. Unfortunately, the person on the other end is as confused as he is. "Carbon credits? Yes, I think we offer something like that... but only if you're growing cover crops and not using synthetic fertilizers. Or maybe it's if you are using synthetic fertilizers but in reduced amounts? Let me check with my supervisor..."

Three phone calls and one headache later, Mr. Patel decides it's not worth the trouble. Instead, he looks into tax incentives. But wait—those only apply if his farm's revenue is above a certain threshold and if he's operating in a designated "climate-resilient farming zone." Which, of course, his farm isn't. And don't even get him started on subsidies. Those seem to be written in a foreign language called "bureaucratese," and require more paperwork than his accountant can manage.

So, what does Mr. Patel do? Probably what most farmers do: shrug it off, stick to what he knows, and hope for the best. Meanwhile, these convoluted financial mechanisms—many of which are well-intentioned—remain inaccessible to the very people they're supposed to help.

Introduction to Climate Finance Mechanisms: A Money Maze to Save the Planet

Climate change may feel like a slow-moving train wreck, but the amount of money moving around to either prevent or deal with it is anything but slow. Global finance has gotten serious about climate, but like everything involving finance, it's complicated—very complicated. From carbon markets to green bonds, climate finance mechanisms are the tools that countries, companies, and individuals are supposed to use to shift the world toward a greener future. And like trying to understand your cable bill, it's often not as straightforward as it should be.

So, what is climate finance, exactly? In the simplest terms, it's the flow of money—public, private, domestic, or international—aimed at reducing greenhouse gas emissions and preparing for the impacts of climate change. The goals can be as varied as funding renewable energy projects, building flood defenses, or helping smallholder farmers adopt more sustainable practices.

Let's put some numbers behind this: According to the Climate Policy Initiative, global climate finance reached $632 billion in 2019-2020. While that might sound like a huge amount (it is), experts argue it's nowhere near enough. The International Energy Agency estimates that in order to meet global climate goals, we need to be investing roughly $4 trillion annually by 2030 in clean energy alone. In other words, we've got a big gap to fill.

But where does this money actually come from, and how does it move through the system? Climate finance comes from three main sources:

Government Budgets: Public money is a big part of the climate finance equation. Governments allocate funds to everything from building infrastructure that can withstand rising sea levels to financing renewable energy projects and providing subsidies for electric vehicles.

Private Sector Investment: Companies and financial institutions are increasingly investing in climate initiatives. Some of this is driven by profit motives (yes, you can make money saving the planet), and some of it is driven by investor and consumer demand for more sustainable practices.

International Aid: For poorer countries, much of their climate finance comes from wealthier nations in the form of development aid, grants, and loans. This is especially crucial for nations that contribute little to global emissions but are most vulnerable to the impacts of climate change. The Paris Agreement set a goal for wealthier nations to mobilize $100 billion annually by 2020 for this purpose. The goal was finally reached in 2022—albeit two years late. Despite hitting the target, many critics argue that the amount is still insufficient to meet the full scope of global climate needs, and that a significant portion of the funds have been allocated as loans rather than grants, adding debt burdens to already vulnerable countries. Additionally, much of the climate finance that has been delivered focuses more on mitigation than adaptation, leaving many nations underprepared for the immediate impacts of climate change.

This delay and imbalance in financing have fueled ongoing discussions about increasing the target and ensuring that future climate finance commitments better reflect the scale and urgency of the crisis, as well as the needs of those most affected.

While these funding sources sound straightforward, the tools used to direct money toward climate initiatives can sometimes resemble a financial labyrinth. Here's a quick look at some of the key mechanisms used to fund climate action:

• *Carbon Markets*: Carbon markets put a price on carbon emissions, allowing companies to trade carbon credits to meet their emissions reduction targets. More on this in the next section, but in essence, companies that reduce their emissions below a certain cap can sell their excess reductions to companies that need them.

• *Green Bonds*: These are bonds issued by companies or governments to raise money for projects that benefit the environment, such as renewable energy installations or energy-efficient infrastructure. Think of it like your usual corporate bond, but with a promise that the proceeds are used to fund something environmentally friendly. Investors love them because they're seen as relatively safe while giving them the satisfaction of contributing to a greener world.

• *Blended Finance*: This is where public and private money come together in what's known as a "blended" approach. Governments or international organizations often use public money to de-risk projects that might be too risky for private investors on their own. For instance, a government might guarantee part of a loan for a solar project, making it more attractive to private investors who wouldn't normally touch it due to the perceived risks.

• *Climate Funds*: There are a number of funds specifically dedicated to climate initiatives. The Green Climate Fund (GCF), created as part of the UN Framework Convention on Climate Change, is one of the largest. It's intended to help developing countries adapt to climate change and transition to greener economies, but—like many things with good intentions—it's often underfunded and caught up in bureaucratic red tape.

• *Tax Incentives and Subsidies*: These are government tools used to encourage businesses and individuals to reduce their emissions. For example, in the U.S., companies can take advantage of tax breaks for installing renewable energy systems or energy-efficient technology. Governments also provide subsidies for electric vehicles, making it more financially feasible for consumers to make greener choices.

So, why aren't we making more progress? One of the biggest barriers is that the mechanisms used to fund climate action, while increasingly sophisticated, are also highly fragmented. You've got governments, corporations, and NGOs all working with different systems and priorities. On top of that, there's still a huge financing gap. Even though global climate finance is increasing year by year, it's not keeping pace with the scale of the problem.

In the coming sections, we'll take a closer look at some of these tools—carbon markets, green bonds, and blended finance—and explore how they work, what challenges they face, and whether they're enough to fund the kind of radical change we need to avoid the worst impacts of climate change. Because, let's be real, $632 billion sounds like a lot until you realize it's a drop in the bucket compared to what's actually needed.

Policy Gaps and Barriers: Where It All Falls Apart

Here's where we come full circle. Despite the countless initiatives, technologies, and finance mechanisms in place, significant policy gaps and barriers remain. One of the biggest issues is the misalignment of incentives. Farmers are often asked to invest in long-term sustainability measures without sufficient short-term support to cover the costs. It's like being handed a recipe book but told you can't use any of the ingredients until you've already baked the cake.

Short-Term Profit vs. Long-Term Sustainability: Policies that incentivize quick returns—like subsidies for monoculture crops—run counter to the need for diversified, resilient agricultural systems. This disjointed approach encourages farmers to maximize yields now, rather than focus on soil health, water conservation, or carbon sequestration.

Lack of Coordination Across Borders: Climate change is a global issue, but most policies are national or regional. This fragmented approach leads to a patchwork of regulations that don't address cross-border issues like water use in shared river basins or migration due to crop failure. It's like building a firebreak that ends at your property line while your neighbor's field burns. Sucks to be you until you realize that fire breaks are only so effective.

Bureaucratic Complexity: The sheer complexity of navigating climate-related programs and incentives makes it difficult for farmers to access the support they need. Programs often require extensive documentation, proof of compliance, and ongoing monitoring that can overwhelm smaller operations. This is not to say proof of compliance isn't a critical part of this effort. So many projects have been plagued by credibility issues that verification has to be a part of these efforts, but the methods for verification should utilize all tools available to make it as cost effective as possible.

Inconsistent Funding: Many initiatives are pilot programs or depend on temporary funding. Farmers who adopt sustainable practices may be left high and dry if funding runs out or policies change with new administrations. With the political seesaw that is the United States, this means that any meaningful investments at the private level really have to come from farmers who have a true sense of obligation to be good stewards of the land. Fortunately, there are many new and multi-generational farmers who understand the importance of stewardship. Unfortunately, there are many politicians who can't even spell the word.

The result? Despite the plethora of policies and technologies, real progress is sluggish. For every step forward, there's often a step back—or at least a very awkward sidestep. And while some farmers and companies are making strides, the overall pace is far too slow to keep up with the rapidly changing climate.

In the next chapter, we'll explore "The Case for Farmers"—why mobilizing the world's farmers is not just a nice idea, but a crucial step in addressing climate change. We'll dive into the untapped potential of sustainable farming and the environmental benefits it can bring, if we can just get the right policies and practices in place. Because if we keep stumbling along as we have been, we're likely to end up with a future where the only thing growing faster than our carbon emissions is our list of regrets.

5
The Case for Farmers

If you've ever wondered who's really on the frontlines of climate change, it's not just the policymakers, corporations, or scientists—it's the farmers...and the polar bears, too, but they have their own books, so we'll focus on the farmers. Think about it: farmers work in close partnership with the land every day, and how they manage that land has far-reaching consequences, not just for their crops, but for the entire planet. Mobilizing the world's farmers to transition to sustainable practices is one of the most powerful levers we can pull in the fight against climate change. Not only does sustainable farming reduce greenhouse gas (GHG) emissions, but it also enhances soil health, improves water management, boosts biodiversity, and even mitigates the risks of wildfires. It can improve air quality, positively impact human health, increase rural income and economic equity and improve food security. This chapter will walk through the environmental benefits of making agriculture a cornerstone of climate action, with hard data and real-world examples to back it up.

Quantifying the Benefits: Just Like the Hips, the Numbers Don't Lie

Greenhouse Gas Reductions

Agriculture is responsible for about 23% of global GHG emissions, primarily from deforestation, methane from livestock and rice cultivation, and nitrous oxide from soil management practices. Sustainable farming techniques like regenerative agriculture, agroforestry, and precision farming have the potential to dramatically cut those emissions. How much? Let's break it down:

Regenerative Agriculture: Practices like crop rotation, cover cropping, and reduced tillage not only sequester carbon in the soil but also reduce the need for synthetic fertilizers, which are a major source of nitrous oxide emissions. It's estimated that regenerative agriculture could sequester up to 23 gigatons of CO_2 by 2050, which would offset roughly 10% of current global emissions annually[23].

Agroforestry: Integrating trees into croplands can store between 1.5 and 2.5 tons of CO_2 per hectare per year. If 10% of the world's farmland adopted agroforestry, it could remove as much as 2.4 billion tons of CO_2 from the atmosphere annually.

Methane Reduction in Livestock: Methane emissions from livestock account for roughly 14.5% of total global GHG emissions[24]. New feed additives (like seaweed) and improved manure management can reduce methane emissions by up to 80% in some cases.

Methane Reduction in Rice Cultivation: Rice cultivation, particularly in flooded fields, is a major source of methane emissions, contributing approximately 10% of total agricultural methane emissions globally. This is due to the anaerobic (oxygen-deprived) conditions in flooded paddies, which promote methane-producing bacteria in the soil.

Fortunately, sustainable water management practices like Alternate Wetting and Drying (AWD) have been developed to significantly reduce methane emissions. By periodically draining the fields, farmers can cut methane emissions by up to 50%, without affecting crop yields. In fact, studies have shown that AWD can also reduce water usage by 30%, making it a win-win for both emissions reduction and resource conservation. It is not, however, a win for the methane producing bacteria. Sorry, guys. If widely adopted, AWD and similar practices could reduce global methane emissions from rice cultivation by as much as 1.26 billion tons of CO_2e annually, representing a substantial mitigation opportunity in a sector responsible for 8-11% of total methane emissions globally.

When you add all these approaches together, you're looking at a 30-50% reduction in global agricultural emissions just through more sustainable farming methods. That works out to a potential reduction of 7-12% of total global emissions.

Soil Health and Carbon Sequestration

Healthy soils do more than just grow better crops—they act as a giant carbon sink. Soil has the capacity to store three times more carbon than the atmosphere, making it a vital part of the climate solution. Practices like no-till farming, crop diversity, and organic amendments can increase the amount of carbon that soil holds, while also making it more resilient to climate shocks like droughts and floods.

Carbon Storage Potential: Some studies estimate that improving soil management on just 15% of the world's agricultural land could store 1 gigaton of CO_2 annually[25].

Yield Improvement: Healthier soils can improve crop yields by 5-10%, which reduces the need for agricultural expansion and deforestation, indirectly reducing carbon emissions from land use change. This is a highly underappreciated aspect of investing in more sustainable agriculture. Let's dive into a hypothetical scenario using Indonesia, an area where I've personally done a lot of work, as an example.

To estimate the potential impact of improved crop yields on avoided emissions from deforestation in Indonesia, we need to look at a few factors: the scale of deforestation for agricultural expansion, the specific crops driving it, and the potential yield improvement from sustainable practices.

Key Factors:

- *Deforestation in Indonesia*: Indonesia is a hotspot for deforestation, primarily due to agricultural expansion for crops like palm oil, rubber, and timber. The World Resources Institute estimates that between 2001 and 2020, Indonesia lost about 28.3 million hectares of tree cover, with an annual deforestation rate of approximately 1 million hectares driven by agricultural expansion . In 2021, deforestation was reported to have declined to around 676,000 hectares due to various conservation efforts, though agricultural expansion remains the primary driver.

- *Crops Driving Deforestation*: Palm oil, rubber, and timber are the largest contributors to deforestation in Indonesia. Palm oil alone accounts for a significant portion of the deforestation. According to the International Union for Conservation of Nature (IUCN), palm oil production in Indonesia contributes to around 270,000 hectares of deforestation per year.

- *Potential Yield Increase*: With a 7.5% yield improvement from healthier soils through sustainable agricultural practices like regenerative farming, this increase would reduce the need for further land conversion. The assumption here is that higher yields would decrease pressure on land expansion, thus avoiding deforestation for crops.

Estimating Avoided Emissions from Deforestation:

Deforestation Emissions:

Tropical deforestation in Indonesia emits significant amounts of CO_2 due to both the loss of trees and the release of carbon stored in peatlands. According to the Global Forest Watch, tropical deforestation in Indonesia releases 1.09 gigatons (Gt) of CO_2 annually, with peatland emissions being a large component.

Impact of Yield Increase:

If yield improvements reduce the need for 7.5% of the land currently being cleared annually for agriculture, this could equate to avoiding 7.5% of deforestation emissions. Assuming deforestation emissions are 1.09 Gt CO_2, then:

Avoided Emissions = 1.09 Gt x 0.075 = 0.08175 Gt or 81.75 million tons CO_2

This means that a 7.5% yield improvement could avoid 81.75 million tons of CO_2 emissions annually in Indonesia alone. Over a decade, this could result in over 800 million tons of avoided CO_2 emissions, which is substantial considering Indonesia's contribution to global emissions through deforestation.

Conclusion: Healthier soils leading to a 7.5% increase in yield for crops like palm oil in Indonesia could result in significant emissions reductions by curbing deforestation. An estimated 81.75 million tons of CO_2 could be avoided annually through better soil management, demonstrating the powerful indirect effects of sustainable agricultural practices on land use and climate change.

These estimates underscore the importance of investing in sustainable agriculture not only for improving crop productivity but also for mitigating global emissions from deforestation.

Water Management

Water, as made popular by that one scene in Cool Hand Luke, is a precious resource, and sustainable farming can help ensure that we don't squander it. Traditional farming often leads to over-irrigation, runoff, and water contamination from fertilizers and pesticides. In contrast, sustainable farming emphasizes water conservation, improving both water quality and quantity.

Water Use Efficiency: Techniques like drip irrigation and smart irrigation systems can reduce water use by up to 50%, helping regions like California and the Middle East cope with water shortages. AWD in rice farming, as mentioned in an earlier chapter, can reduce water usage in rice paddies by 30% with no need for capital investment or technology to implement.

Groundwater Recharge: Practices like cover cropping and reduced tillage help improve the soil's ability to retain water, which boosts groundwater levels and reduces the need for irrigation. This is particularly important in areas with increasing populations where development is leading to greater strains on the existing water table.

Pollution Reduction: By reducing the use of synthetic fertilizers and pesticides, sustainable farming cuts down on the runoff that contaminates rivers, lakes, and oceans. This has a significant impact on downstream communities of humans and animals. The funny thing about ecosystems is that they are somewhat interconnected so when you make a major change to one part, it has a big impact on all the others.

A great example of the interconnectedness of ecosystems and the impact of sustainable farming on pollution reduction is the Gulf of Mexico Dead Zone, which sounds like Panama City Beach two weeks after spring break ends, but is actually one of the largest hypoxic (low oxygen) areas in the world. This "dead zone" is largely a result of nutrient pollution from agricultural runoff in the Mississippi River Basin. The use of synthetic fertilizers, especially nitrogen and phosphorus, in upstream farms leads to excess nutrients being washed into rivers and eventually into the Gulf. This nutrient overload causes massive algal blooms. When the algae die and decompose, they deplete oxygen levels in the water, leading to hypoxia—conditions in which most marine life cannot survive.

This process significantly disrupts the Gulf's ecosystem, causing fish kills and harming the commercial fishing industry that many communities depend on. Something Forrest Gump would not be happy about. Sustainable farming practices like reducing synthetic fertilizer use, implementing cover cropping, and maintaining buffer strips along waterways can significantly reduce nutrient runoff. For instance, a study by the U.S. Geological Survey (USGS) found that nutrient load reductions of just 20-30% in the Mississippi River Basin could result in a substantial decrease in the size of the hypoxic zone in the Gulf.

A double whammy for the Dead Zone is that because it is an oxygen-deprived environment, when the algae die and decompose, it releases methane and nitrous oxide into the atmosphere, both very potent GHG's. This results in a net-negative affect for the climate.

This shows how changing farming practices in one region can have cascading benefits for ecosystems hundreds of miles downstream, ultimately protecting marine life, improving water quality, and supporting human livelihoods that depend on those ecosystems.

Biodiversity

Sustainable farming doesn't just protect plants and animals—it actively encourages biodiversity. Monocultures (growing the same crop over and over) deplete soil nutrients and reduce habitat for wildlife, while diversified farms foster ecosystems that are rich in plant and animal life.

Pollinator Support: Farms that implement agroecological practices such as planting cover crops, maintaining flower strips, and reducing pesticide use can see a significant boost in pollinator populations—particularly bees—by as much as 25-30%. Pollinators are crucial for the fertilization of many crops, including fruits, vegetables, and nuts. Around 75% of global food crops depend, at least in part, on pollination, which means that supporting pollinator populations directly impacts food security. Beyond food production, bees and other pollinators play a vital role in maintaining healthy ecosystems by promoting biodiversity. The decline of pollinators due to habitat loss, pesticide use, and monocultures has already triggered global concerns, so integrating agroecological practices helps reverse this trend and can lead to healthier, more resilient farms.

By creating environments that attract pollinators, farms not only enhance crop yields but also contribute to the stability of ecosystems that are dependent on these species. This leads to a positive feedback loop where healthier pollinator populations help sustain not only the farm's productivity but also the broader biodiversity that supports soil health, water quality, and pest control.

Wildlife Habitats: Sustainable agricultural practices such as agroforestry, field margins, and hedgerows can create crucial habitats for wildlife, including birds, mammals, and beneficial insects. Agroforestry integrates trees with crops and livestock systems, which enhances biodiversity by providing shelter, food, and breeding grounds for many species. Field margins—small strips of land at the edges of cultivated fields—allow for natural flora to thrive, which in turn supports wildlife populations that help regulate pests naturally.

The importance of this is twofold. First, by maintaining wildlife habitats, farms benefit from natural pest control provided by predators such as birds and predatory insects. This reduces the need for chemical pesticides, which not only cuts costs for farmers but also mitigates the environmental impact of chemical runoff into nearby water bodies. Second, these habitats contribute to ecosystem balance, maintaining biodiversity that supports ecosystem services like pollination, water filtration, and nutrient cycling. The inclusion of wildlife-friendly practices also strengthens the overall resilience of farms to climate change, pests, and diseases, making them more sustainable in the long term.

Both pollinator support and wildlife habitats highlight how a holistic approach to farming—one that recognizes the interconnectedness of ecosystems—can lead to more productive, resilient, and environmentally friendly agriculture. This is totally why I have large patches of uncontrolled weeds, wildflowers and brambles on my own small farm. It has nothing to do with my lack of attention to detail or farming ineptitude.

Expanding the Lens: Beyond GHGs

While the benefits of sustainable farming for GHG reductions are clear, the positive impacts go well beyond just lowering carbon emissions. Let's take a look at other gains.

Wildfire Mitigation

As climate change drives hotter and drier conditions, wildfires are becoming more frequent and more severe. A single wildfire can undo decades of conservation and sequestration activity. Not to mention the economic, psychological, physiological and social impact these fires can have. But sustainable farming can play a role in reducing this risk.

Buffer Zones: Agroforestry and hedgerows create natural barriers that slow the spread of wildfires, reducing their intensity and protecting both crops and surrounding ecosystems.

Soil Moisture Retention: Healthy soils retain more moisture, which reduces the risk of wildfires spreading through dry fields or forests.

Active Fire Mitigation: Several programs exist to encourage active wildfire mitigation through forest litter cleanup, improved forest management, and improved rangeland management practices. These are all part of a comprehensive sustainable agricultural approach, especially in the ranch and rangeland side of agriculture. Carbon credits, tax breaks, insurance premium reductions, and direct government subsidies help drive this activity in some parts of the world.

Air Quality

Agricultural practices, particularly livestock farming and fertilizer application, can significantly impact air quality by releasing ammonia, methane, and other harmful pollutants into the atmosphere. Crop residue burning is known to release small particulate matter in the air, colloquially referred to as PM2.5 (for the particle size), which can cause smog and major respiratory and other health conditions. By adopting sustainable practices, farmers can help reduce these emissions:

Reduced Fertilizer Use: Organic farming methods, which minimize synthetic fertilizer use, can reduce emissions of nitrous oxide, a key contributor to smog and acid rain.

Methane Reduction: As mentioned earlier, new livestock management techniques can reduce methane emissions, improving air quality and contributing to better public health outcomes.

PM2.5 Reduction: Crop residue burning, particularly in regions like Southeast Asia and parts of India, is a major source of PM2.5—a fine particulate matter that poses severe risks to respiratory health. PM2.5 particles are small enough to penetrate deep into the lungs, causing or exacerbating conditions such as asthma, bronchitis, and even cardiovascular issues. By adopting alternative methods of crop residue management, such as no-till farming, mulching, or using crop residues for bioenergy or biochar production, farmers can drastically reduce PM2.5 emissions. This is not only beneficial for the health of nearby communities but also plays a significant role in improving overall air quality.

Reducing these pollutants doesn't just improve public health—it also leads to clearer skies, mitigating the formation of smog and contributing to better visibility and a healthier ecosystem. These air quality improvements are directly tied to sustainable farming practices and show how integrated approaches to agriculture can have far-reaching positive outcomes for both people and the environment.

Regional Case Studies

To better understand the environmental benefits, let's take a closer look at regions where sustainable farming practices have already made an impact:

California: Sustainable farming methods, such as drip irrigation, have helped farmers in the drought-prone Central Valley reduce water usage by up to 40%, while also increasing crop yields. Farmers who've adopted cover cropping and reduced tillage are also seeing improved soil health, which has helped buffer against climate extremes like droughts and floods. Adoption of wildfire mitigation practices for ranches is another major opportunity for California agriculture to make a significant environmental impact.

Mekong Delta: In Vietnam, rice farmers using Alternate Wetting and Drying (AWD) techniques have reduced water usage by 30% and cut methane emissions by nearly 50%. In trial farms in Kien Giang Province, where this was coupled with a nano-fertilizer that enhanced nutrient uptake from a company called BSB Nanotechnology, the results showed a significant increase in yield in addition to the methane reduction, water savings and reduced chemical leaching. Total yield increase ranged from 15% to 25%, reaching up to 10 tons per hectare. The combination of practices also reduced chemical fertilizer use by 15% and pesticide application by 20%.

Sub-Saharan Africa: In Niger, farmers implemented "farmer-managed natural regeneration" (FMNR), a widely recognized method for restoring degraded land through agroecological practices. This approach has helped farmers in Niger restore over 5 million hectares of land by encouraging the regrowth of trees and shrubs from existing root systems, improving soil fertility, reducing erosion, and increasing agricultural yields.

This initiative, often referred to as the "Regreening of the Sahel," has boosted food security in a region prone to desertification and climate challenges. The key to FMNR's success lies in its simplicity, low cost, and ability to regenerate tree cover without the need for new planting. It allows for sustainable agricultural productivity while rehabilitating degraded land. As a result, yields have improved, and the region has seen reduced vulnerability to droughts[26].

Economic and Social Impact: Monetizing Sustainable Agriculture for Smallholder Farmers in the Global South

The transition to sustainable agriculture offers a transformative opportunity for smallholder farmers and farm-adjacent communities, especially in the Global South, to not only enhance environmental outcomes but also unlock significant economic benefits. By incorporating new revenue streams, creating business opportunities, and improving gender equality, sustainable agriculture becomes a key driver of socio-economic justice. Let's dive into how it can accomplish that in the next section.

Creating Diverse Revenue Streams

One of the most exciting aspects of sustainable agriculture for smallholder farmers is the potential for monetization through environmental services like carbon credits, carbon offsets, and carbon insets. Smallholder farmers, many of whom operate on the frontlines of climate vulnerability, can transition from traditional farming practices to ones that sequester carbon, reduce greenhouse gas emissions, and improve soil health. These practices— ranging from agroforestry and regenerative agriculture to soil carbon sequestration—create opportunities for farmers to sell carbon credits and access premium markets for sustainably grown commodities. Some of these methods are capital intensive but some require little to no cash investment, making them very accessible as long as the training and support is available.

Example: Carbon Insetting for Direct Revenue

If you are a corporate sustainability executive and your company operates ANYWHERE in the agricultural supply chain…pay attention. Carbon insetting, where corporations within the supply chain fund sustainable practices to offset their emissions (typically scope 3 emissions), enables smallholder farmers to earn additional income without needing a third-party intermediary. This decentralized approach connects farmers directly to buyers, often bypassing middlemen who traditionally take a cut of the profits. Multinational companies are increasingly looking for opportunities to source sustainably and use insets to meet their carbon goals, opening the door for smallholder farmers to access international markets and increase their earnings. This can drive significant income growth for the farmer, in some cases up to 20%. It also makes a huge social impact for the company sponsoring it. The money paid to the farmer to switch to sustainable practices is not just reducing the company's scope 3 footprint, it's also helping alleviate poverty, increase food security, improve water and air quality and, in many cases, support gender equality. Not to be cynical, but the marketing return on investment for this type of initiative cannot be beaten by any other carbon reduction program that I am aware of. And the kicker is that insetting is a much more defensible strategy for carbon reduction than most other plans. You are literally reducing the carbon footprint of the products and services you provide so even though most rabid climate activists will have a hard time finding fault with this approach.

New Business Opportunities in the Sustainability Space

Sustainable agriculture also fosters new entrepreneurial opportunities. The demand for local suppliers who can provide inputs for sustainable farming, such as organic fertilizers, biochar, and eco-friendly pest management solutions, is growing. These businesses can serve both local and export markets, creating new jobs and stimulating rural economies. Entrepreneurs can also take advantage of emerging technologies, such as precision agriculture tools or blockchain-based traceability systems, which support sustainable farming practices by helping farmers track and verify their environmental impact, making their products more marketable in global sustainability markets.

Impact on Farm-Adjacent Workers

In addition to direct farm work, new roles are emerging in

logistics, technical services, and sustainability consulting—fields that are particularly attractive to younger workers and those looking to diversify income streams away from purely agricultural labor. These emerging job markets create a sustainable employment base within farming communities, reducing rural-to-urban migration and promoting local economic development.

Premium Commodity Pricing

Consumers are increasingly willing to pay a premium for sustainably produced goods, which drives higher market prices for products like organic coffee, fair-trade chocolate, or eco-friendly textiles. This demand incentivizes smallholder farmers to adopt sustainable practices, improving not only their financial stability but also their environmental footprint. For example, farmers who use regenerative agricultural methods or agroecological systems can access niche markets where buyers pay above-average prices for commodities labeled as environmentally or ethically produced.

Example: Premium Market Access in Coffee Production

In countries like Ethiopia and Colombia, smallholder coffee farmers who practice organic or shade-grown coffee farming have been able to tap into premium markets, securing prices 30-50% higher than those for conventionally grown coffee. These premiums reflect not only consumer demand but also recognition of the environmental benefits, such as biodiversity conservation and reduced chemical inputs, which come with sustainable practices.

Gender Equality and Empowerment

A significant portion of the farms in the Global South are operated by women. This phenomenon is tied to a broader socio-economic trend known as the "feminization of agriculture." This shift happens when men from rural households migrate to cities or other regions for seasonal or permanent work, often in industries like construction, manufacturing, or the gig economy. This leaves women responsible for managing both household and agricultural activities.

In many regions of sub-Saharan Africa, South Asia, and Southeast Asia, male migration for employment is common, leading women to take on the role of primary agricultural laborers and decision-makers. This trend is especially pronounced in areas where urbanization and industrialization are drawing male laborers into low-skilled, city-based jobs, often resulting in a seasonal or long-term shift in gender roles on the farm. The rise of the gig economy has only hastened this trend.

According to research by the Food and Agriculture Organization (FAO), women account for approximately 50% of the agricultural workforce in many developing countries. In certain regions, such as South Asia and sub-Saharan Africa, women's labor contribution to agriculture can exceed 60%. Moreover, this feminization of agriculture has created both opportunities and challenges for women. While it allows women to gain more autonomy in decision-making, it also exposes them to a heavier burden, particularly given the lack of access to resources, credit, and training that male farmers more easily receive.

The feminization of agriculture in the Global South is not just a reflection of gender dynamics but also of broader economic and labor trends. Women's growing involvement in farm operations creates new avenues for policy interventions aimed at improving access to finance, training, and land rights for women, which can help mitigate the challenges they face in agricultural sustainability efforts. Programs that facilitate access to carbon markets, sustainable certification schemes, and direct farm-to-consumer sales help ensure that women benefit from the shift to sustainable farming.

Example: Empowering Women in Africa's Shea Butter Supply Chain

In West Africa, the shea butter industry—dominated by women producers—has seen increased access to global markets for sustainable, fair-trade products. By adopting agroforestry and organic farming practices, women farmers have not only improved their yields and environmental impact but have also secured higher prices and long-term partnerships with ethical brands in the cosmetics and food sectors. This success is a testament to how sustainable agriculture can contribute to gender equity and economic empowerment.

Secondary Economic Impacts and Community Development

The ripple effects of monetizing sustainable agriculture extend beyond the farm. When farmers earn higher incomes, they reinvest in their local communities—purchasing goods, employing workers, and stimulating rural economies. In many cases, sustainable farming initiatives also foster community-based cooperatives, which can collectively negotiate better prices, access financing, and share resources to lower input costs. As these practices scale, the cumulative effect leads to enhanced food security, improved livelihoods, and greater social cohesion.

Example: Secondary Financial Impact in Southeast Asia

In Vietnam's Mekong Delta, farmers transitioning to alternate wetting and drying (AWD) techniques in rice cultivation not only benefit from direct methane reduction payments through carbon credits but also generate significant water savings. The additional income has enabled farmers to diversify into aquaculture and agrotourism, further stabilizing local economies and reducing reliance on traditional monocrop agriculture. This is critical as the region has also seen an influx of brackish water leading to reduced yields and quality in certain areas over recent years due to sea level and other environmental changes. In fact, the Mekong Delta is one of the most vulnerable regions in the world to climate change, with saltwater intrusion threatening both agriculture and freshwater availability. Farmers in the region have been forced to adopt various adaptive strategies, including shifting to more salt-tolerant crops or diversifying into aquaculture. This adaptation has become increasingly critical as brackish water intrusion reduces the land available for traditional rice cultivation, which has been the backbone of the region's economy. But, thanks to the advancements highlighted here and the additional revenue they generate, it has improved community-wide access to essential services like healthcare and education by bolstering local financial resources.

A Path to Economic Justice

By reducing the reliance on intermediaries and enabling farmers to directly monetize their sustainable practices, sustainable agriculture provides an unprecedented opportunity for economic justice. Traditionally, smallholder farmers in the Global South have been marginalized in global markets, trapped in a cycle of debt and exploitation by middlemen who control access to inputs and financing. The digital nature of sustainability-driven markets, whether through blockchain-backed carbon credits or transparent insetting arrangements, allows farmers to reclaim power in these value chains. By aligning environmental stewardship with direct financial incentives, sustainable agriculture offers a pathway to greater economic equity and resilience in the most vulnerable communities.

The transition to sustainable agriculture represents a significant opportunity to uplift smallholder farmers and farm-adjacent workers in the Global South. By creating diverse revenue streams, fostering new business opportunities, and addressing gender equality, sustainable farming practices serve as a catalyst for both environmental protection and socio-economic empowerment. As the world continues to seek solutions to the global climate crisis, smallholder farmers stand at the forefront of a revolution that could reshape economies, strengthen communities, and drive meaningful progress toward a more equitable and sustainable future.

Humanizing the Data: Real Stories, Real Impact

Behind every data point is a farmer who is living the reality of climate change—and fighting back. Take Uncle Lek, a smallholder farmer in Thailand who, through a program with a regional company: Net Zero Carbon, switched to sustainable farming after years of watching his soil degrade under chemical-intensive practices and traditional rice paddy flooding. Since adopting regenerative

agriculture, his yields have improved by 20%, his water use has decreased by 40%, and he's selling surplus carbon credits to supplement his income. This has allowed him to invest in better equipment, which makes him more efficient, and his net income has increased significantly. This increase is felt throughout his village and more of his neighbors have made the switch as well.

Conclusion: The Green Revolution, Reimagined

The data is compelling, but the message is even clearer: farmers have the power to reshape the future of our planet. By transitioning to sustainable cultivation practices, we can reduce GHG emissions, improve soil health, conserve water, and protect biodiversity—all while ensuring that farming remains a viable livelihood. Sustainable farming isn't just about fighting climate change; it's about creating a resilient food system that can weather the environmental and economic challenges of the 21st century. But what does this mean for the rest of us? We'll take a look at that in the next chapter.

6
The Impact On the Rest of Us

Hopefully, my heartfelt case for farmers struck home and you've already begun researching where to send your check. But if you're not quite there yet, you may be wondering, "Okay, but how does all this sustainable farming business affect me?" Excellent question, dear reader, and let me reassure you—sustainable farming has a ripple effect that extends far beyond the field, impacting the entire supply chain, big corporations, and ultimately, you (yes, you!) as a consumer. Let's peel back the organic, non-GMO, sustainably sourced onion and see how that works.

Quick Shoutout: Speaking of sustainably sourced onions, a lot of the work going on in the sustainability space in agriculture is not getting much attention. An example of this is Bland Farms, one of the largest onion growers in the southeastern US. Over the last few years, Bland has invested heavily in reducing the carbon footprint of their packing facility and improving the sustainability of their packaging. They fully electrified their fleet of forklifts and in-facility vehicles, substantially increased insulation and reorganized packing and storage to optimize energy efficiency. They have begun installing solar to make the facility energy independent and are working to shorten and optimize planting and harvest routes to minimize fuel usage. While one motivator is their role as good stewards of the land they've farmed for generations, the changes make good business sense, too.

Supply Chain Dynamics: From Soil to Store Shelves

At first glance, what happens on a farm might seem worlds apart from the products that land on store shelves. However, the farm is the start of so many things in the supply chain, and small changes at the soil level can lead to significant improvements throughout.

Let's say a farmer switches to regenerative practices like cover cropping and reduced tillage. Healthier soil leads to better water retention, improved biodiversity, and—here's the big one—increased crop yields. Now, what does this mean for the supply chain?

Higher Yields, Lower Losses: With healthier soils, crops not only grow better, but they are also more resilient to pests and diseases, leading to higher yields. When a farmer produces more, manufacturers further down the chain receive a more consistent supply, reducing the risk of shortages or price spikes due to crop failure. Think of it as a buffer zone between you and those dreaded "price hikes" on your frosted flakes.

Less Waste: Healthier crops also mean fewer losses during storage and transportation. Fruits and vegetables are less likely to rot or get damaged when they've been grown in optimal conditions. For companies in the business of food production, this reduction in waste means they don't have to overcompensate by purchasing or producing more than they need—saving everyone money. In short, your weekly grocery haul might cost you less, and you'll have fewer mushy apples to deal with at the bottom of the bag.

Example time: In the coffee industry, regenerative farming has not only improved yields but also reduced bean spoilage during transport. Healthier soil supports the growth of stronger plants with more nutrient-dense beans, reducing the amount of rejected or wasted coffee during processing. This has directly lowered costs for coffee brands—and consequently, your morning latte is a few cents cheaper.

Scope 3 Emissions and Beyond: What's in it for CEOs and CFOs?

Let's face it, CEOs and CFOs aren't going to be swayed by the warm fuzzies of saving the planet. No, they want cold, hard numbers—preferably ones that look good on a sustainability report or, even better, in the company's bottom line. So, here's the kicker: sustainable farming practices can help them with something they're increasingly being held accountable for—Scope 3 emissions.

For those blissfully unaware, Scope 3 emissions refer to the indirect emissions that occur throughout a company's value chain. This includes everything from the emissions generated by suppliers (hello, farms!) to the shipping of raw materials, all the way to the emissions produced when consumers use a product (think of all that water it takes to brew a cup of coffee). These emissions typically account for a whopping 70-80% of a company's total carbon footprint. No wonder CEOs and CFOs get a little twitchy when they hear the words "Scope 3."

Fun Fact: Sneaking up behind a CEO and shouting 'Scope 3' could possibly make them scream like a little baby. It could also get you fired if it's your CEO...and it's in the middle of a Board meeting.

Here's where sustainable farming comes in. By reducing the carbon footprint of the very first stage of the supply chain (i.e., what happens on the farm), companies can significantly cut down on their Scope 3 emissions. That means fewer emissions to report, a shinier sustainability report, and a happier board of directors. Win-win!

It's worth noting that Scope 3 works both upstream and downstream. If your product is used on the farm, like fertilizer, for example, then that application is also taken into account as part of your Scope 3 footprint. In fact, it is estimated that up to 2/3rds of a fertilizer company's entire carbon footprint occurs when their product is applied on the field.

Example: Take Nestlé, a company that's taken aggressive steps to reduce Scope 3 emissions by sourcing coffee beans from farms practicing regenerative agriculture. By partnering directly with these farms, they reduce their carbon footprint, gain valuable sustainability certifications, and avoid regulatory penalties for excessive emissions.

But the real kicker? It can actually save money in the long run. More efficient supply chains mean lower operating costs, reduced exposure to environmental risks, and better pricing leverage. Plus, consumers are increasingly willing to pay a premium for products labeled as sustainable (more on this later). So, CEOs, if you're not yet convinced, just remember: lower emissions, higher profits, and the ability to brag about being environmentally responsible. What's not to love?

Consumer Impact: What's in it for Me?

Now, onto the part you've been waiting for—how does this affect your day-to-day life? Imagine you're at the grocery store, staring down an apple. Staring back at you, it looks shinier, redder, and—dare I say—crisper than the apples you've encountered in the past. Turns out, it's grown using sustainable farming practices. Why should you care?

Better Quality Products: Healthier soils mean healthier crops. That apple in your hand isn't just a visual delight— it's likely more nutritious, too. Studies have shown that produce from farms practicing regenerative agriculture often contains higher levels of vitamins, minerals, and antioxidants compared to conventionally grown produce. This is because healthier soils are better at retaining nutrients, leading to crops with enhanced nutritional profiles. While you might pay a little more upfront, think of the long-term health benefits and potential savings on healthcare costs down the road. So, even though that apple might be a few cents pricier, you're getting more bang for your buck in terms of nutrients.

Lower Prices Over Time: Here's where it gets a bit more nuanced. While sustainable farming practices can help reduce costs for farmers by improving crop resilience and cutting down on inputs like synthetic fertilizers, these savings don't always immediately translate to lower prices for consumers. Why? Because the initial costs of transitioning to sustainable methods—such as certification fees, new equipment, or training—often mean farmers need to charge more initially.

However, over time, as more farmers adopt sustainable practices and as supply chains become more efficient, prices could stabilize. It's not a short-term fix, but in the long run, these practices can reduce the volatility of food prices by making crops more resilient to climate extremes and reducing dependence on external inputs. So, while the "trickle-down effect" may take a while, sustainable farming helps create more stable food prices in the long run. The potential for price reductions may be modest but tangible as adoption scales. Or, at the very least, it could reduce the impact of inflation for these commodities over time.

Feel Good Purchases: In addition to the tangible benefits of buying sustainable products, there's a deeper layer of value that speaks directly to the customer's "philosophical problem"—an idea emphasized in the StoryBrand® marketing framework. This concept refers to the larger moral or existential question a customer is wrestling with when making a purchase. In this case, the philosophical problem could be: Am I doing my part to support a sustainable, healthier planet?

When you purchase a sustainably grown apple, you're addressing this inner conflict by making a choice that aligns with your values. You're not just buying food; you're affirming your commitment to environmental stewardship. This creates a strong emotional connection between the consumer and the product because it's not just solving a need for nourishment—it's solving a moral need to live in line with personal values.

For companies, framing their products as a solution to this philosophical problem can be powerful. It goes beyond functionality or price and taps into the emotional desire for purpose and meaning. You, the consumer, aren't just eating an apple—you're contributing to the fight against climate change, supporting ethical farming, and promoting biodiversity. It's a small action that ties into a much larger narrative about creating a better world, allowing you to feel like an active participant in a global movement.

That sense of purposeful consumption adds value to the experience, and smart brands can leverage this in their storytelling. The product becomes a symbol of the consumer's heroic journey, making each purchase feel like a meaningful step toward their ideal self. Buying that sustainably grown apple may not solve climate change overnight, but it's part of a larger movement with real global impacts. Supporting farmers who prioritize sustainability means you're helping reduce GHG emissions, conserve water, and preserve biodiversity—all while enjoying a fresh snack. And honestly, isn't it nice to feel like you're making a positive difference, one bite at a time?

In short, while sustainable farming might not always lead to immediate cost savings for consumers, it has the potential to deliver long-term benefits, not just for your wallet, but for your health and the planet too.

Case Study Examples: Sustainability in Action

To bring this all together, let's look at a few real-world examples of how sustainable farming has transformed supply chains and created new opportunities.

Unilever and Tea Sourcing: Unilever, through its popular tea brands like Lipton, has been working with Rainforest Alliance-certified farms for years. By focusing on sustainable farming, they've seen reduced water usage and improved biodiversity on tea farms in Kenya and India. Not only has this reduced their Scope 3 emissions, but it's also created a more resilient supply chain. Droughts and erratic weather patterns now pose less of a risk to their operations, and they've even marketed these benefits to eco-conscious consumers, leading to higher sales in some regions.

Danone's Regenerative Dairy Supply Chain: Danone has partnered with dairy farms to transition to regenerative practices like rotational grazing and reduced antibiotic use. These changes have led to healthier cows (who knew cows could look so sprightly?) and better milk yields. As a result, Danone's dairy products are less likely to suffer from price fluctuations due to supply chain disruptions, and they've cut down on their Scope 3 emissions, which are significant in the dairy industry.

Patagonia's Regenerative Cotton: Known for its commitment to sustainability, Patagonia sources cotton from farms using regenerative agriculture methods.

This not only improves soil health but also reduces the need for synthetic fertilizers, lowering the brand's overall environmental impact. What's more, Patagonia has built a marketing campaign around its sustainability efforts, turning its ethical sourcing into a competitive advantage that resonates with its eco-conscious customers.

Wrapping It Up

So, what's the impact of sustainable farming on the rest of us? A lot more than you might think. From creating a more resilient and efficient supply chain to reducing the carbon footprints of the world's biggest companies to delivering healthier and better-quality products to your table, the ripple effects of sustainable agriculture touch everyone.

In the next chapter, we'll wade into the wide world of sustainable agriculture practices, examining what's realistic versus idealistic and trying to figure out what's stopping us from just doing it already!

7
The Nitty Gritty Dirt...Stuff

Welcome to the part of the journey where we roll up our sleeves, dig into the dirt (literally), and get our hands dirty with the actual practices that make sustainable farming tick. Think of this chapter as your recipe book for the green feast we're all aiming to cook up. We'll break down the different sustainable farming techniques, explore the hurdles farmers face in adopting them, rank these practices by feasibility, and take a peek into the future of agricultural innovation. Let's get cooking!

Breaking Down Practices: From Seed to Sustainability

Sustainable farming isn't a one-size-fits-all hat—it's more like a wardrobe full of versatile outfits, each suited to different climates, crops, and farmer preferences. Here are some of the star players in the sustainable farming arena:

No-Till Farming: The Lazy Gardener's Dream
Brief History:

No-till farming traces its roots back to the 1940s but gained significant traction in the 1970s as a response to soil erosion problems. It revolutionized agriculture by challenging the traditional plow-and-seed model.

Scientific Backing:

By leaving the soil undisturbed, no-till farming enhances soil structure, increases water retention, and boosts microbial activity. Studies have shown that no-till practices can reduce soil erosion by up to 90% and increase carbon sequestration, making it a powerhouse for both productivity and the planet.

Practical Implementation Advice:

Start by investing in no-till equipment like specialized seed drills. Transition gradually—maybe no-till one field at a time—to allow your soil (and your crops) to adjust. Keep an eye on weed management, as no-till can sometimes invite a more robust weed population initially. Partnering with local agricultural extension services can provide the support and training needed to make the switch smoother than a well-ironed shirt.

Quick Plug for Agricultural Extension: While not available everywhere, many states in the US and other countries offer extension services to farmers, gardeners and others at no cost. I am admittedly a little biased, but the University of Georgia's Cooperative Extension service is an incredible resource with agents in every county of the state and specialists in some of the state's most important focus areas. Their expertise goes beyond traditional row crops to include home gardens, urban agriculture, food, health & nutrition, home economics and home financial planning, as well as environmental and natural resources.

Cover Cropping: Nature's Own Mulch
Brief History:

Cover cropping has been around for centuries, with ancient civilizations using legumes and grasses to protect and enrich their fields. It saw a resurgence in the 20th century as sustainable practices gained momentum.

Scientific Backing:

Cover crops prevent soil erosion, improve soil fertility by fixing nitrogen, and enhance water infiltration. Research indicates that cover cropping can increase organic matter in the soil by 10-20%, leading to healthier, more productive fields.

Practical Implementation Advice:

Choose cover crops that complement your main crops—legumes like clover or grasses like rye are popular choices. Plant them during the off-season or between cash crops. Ensure timely termination (cutting them down) to prevent competition with your main crops. It's like having a green roommate who cleans up after themselves and even brings some extra veggies to the table.

Alternate Wetting and Drying (AWD): The Rice Farmer's Secret Sauce

Brief History:

Rice farmers have been following forced drying for hundreds of years, although it typically didn't yield the same positive results we see today. Planned AWD was developed in the early 2000s as a water-saving technique for rice cultivation in several parts of South and Southeast Asia, with its fastest adoption in the Philippines. It has since spread globally as a proven method to reduce methane emissions and conserve water.

Scientific Backing:

AWD reduces methane emissions by up to 50% and cuts water usage by around 30%. It maintains or even improves rice yields, making it a win-win for farmers and the environment. Studies from the International Rice Research Institute (IRRI) confirm these benefits, highlighting AWD's role in sustainable rice production. I can personally attest to this as we have worked with thousands of farmers to successfully transition to AWD and reap the benefits of the system. I'd be happy to introduce you to several thousand happy farmers who can back me up. (And one unhappy farmer named Pae. It was an accident, Pae, I said I would buy you a new one.)

Practical Implementation Advice:

Implement AWD by periodically draining your rice paddies instead of keeping them continuously flooded. This requires careful water management and monitoring, so investing in reliable irrigation infrastructure is key. We recommend installing a "pani pipe" in the field to ensure the proper levels of irrigation are maintained. Pani pipes are generally six-inch diameter PVC pipes with holes drilled in them that are partially buried in the soil. It allows the farmer to see the water level below ground level so that they can reflood the field when the water reaches 15cm below ground level. Training and support from agricultural extension services, carbon project developers, or companies like Spiro Carbon can help farmers transition smoothly. Think of it as giving your rice paddies a spa day—just the right amount of hydration without overdoing it.

Agroforestry: The Tree-Crop Meet Cute

Brief History:

Agroforestry has ancient origins, with traditional systems in Africa, Asia, and Latin America integrating trees into agricultural landscapes. For example, indigenous farming practices in Central America have long incorporated trees to create shade for crops and maintain soil fertility. In sub-Saharan Africa, communities used trees to enhance nutrient cycles and provide fodder, fuel, and food. Modern agroforestry gained prominence in the late 20th century as a strategy for sustainable land use, particularly after recognition by international organizations such as the FAO and World Agroforestry Centre (ICRAF). It is now viewed as a critical component of climate resilience and biodiversity conservation, especially in regions vulnerable

to deforestation and land degradation.
Scientific Backing:

Integrating trees with crops enhances biodiversity, improves soil health, and sequesters carbon. Studies show that agroforestry systems can store between 1.5 and 2.5 tons of CO_2 per hectare annually, making them significant players in climate mitigation.
Practical Implementation Advice:

Start by selecting tree species that complement your crops and climate. Incorporate trees into field margins, alley cropping systems, or silvopasture (trees with livestock). Manage tree density to ensure they don't overshadow your crops. Regular pruning and maintenance are essential to balance tree and crop growth. It's like adding a tall friend to your group—great for shade and your Saturday pickup game, but you've got to keep them from hogging all the spotlight.

Crop Rotation and Intercropping: Mixing It Up
Brief History:

Crop rotation and intercropping have been essential agricultural methods for millennia, dating back to ancient civilizations in Europe, Africa, and Asia, where they were used to maintain soil fertility and control pests. These techniques saw a resurgence in the 20th century with the rise of sustainable agriculture. While two-crop systems like corn and soybeans are still common, more diverse rotations that include legumes, grains, and cover crops offer greater benefits by enhancing nutrient cycling, reducing soil erosion, and promoting biodiversity. Modern sustainable practices emphasize the value of integrating a wider variety of crops to improve long-term soil health and resilience.
Scientific Backing:

Rotating different crops disrupts pest and disease cycles, reduces soil nutrient depletion, and enhances soil structure. Intercropping, the practice of growing two or more crops together, can increase overall productivity and biodiversity. Research indicates that these practices can boost yields by 10-15% and improve resilience to climate extremes.

Practical Implementation Advice:

Plan your crop cycles to include a variety of plants that complement each other. For example, rotate nitrogen-fixing legumes with nitrogen-demanding cereals. In intercropping, pair crops that occupy different niches—like planting corn with beans and squash (the classic "Three Sisters" method). Effective planning and record-keeping are essential to maximize benefits and minimize competition between crops. It's like hosting a dinner party where each guest brings something unique to the table—diversity leads to a more vibrant and enjoyable feast.

Barriers to Adoption: Hurdles on the Green Path

You can see there are lots of benefits to adopting these strategies. So why isn't everyone doing it already? Well, adopting sustainable farming practices isn't as simple as flipping a switch. Farmers face a variety of obstacles that can make the transition challenging:

Initial Costs

Switching to sustainable practices often requires upfront investment in new equipment, seeds, or infrastructure. For example, no-till farming might require specialized seed drills, and agroforestry could mean planting thousands of trees. These initial costs can be daunting, especially for smallholder farmers operating on tight margins.

Lack of Technical Knowledge

Sustainable farming techniques can be complex and require specific knowledge and skills. Farmers may need training and support to implement practices like AWD or agroforestry effectively. Without access to extension services or educational resources, the learning curve can be steep.

Risk-Averse Nature of Farming

Farming is inherently risky, and many farmers are hesitant to adopt new practices that could potentially disrupt their established routines or lead to unforeseen challenges. With many farmers only getting one major crop per year, they only get so many "at bats" in their career. The fear of crop failure or yield loss during the transition period can make farmers stick with conventional methods, even if they're less sustainable.

Access to Financing

Many sustainable practices require financial resources that farmers might not have. Access to credit, subsidies, or grants can be limited, particularly in developing regions. Without financial support, the cost barrier becomes insurmountable.

Market Access

For sustainable practices to be economically viable, there needs to be a market willing to pay a premium for sustainably grown products. Farmers may struggle to find buyers or may not receive fair prices for their sustainable produce, making the transition less attractive.

Realistic Assessment: Cooking Up Sustainability with a Dash of Reality

Let's rank these sustainable farming practices by feasibility using a fun culinary analogy—comparing them to cooking techniques. Some are as easy as boiling an egg, while others are as delicate and expensive as baking a soufflé. Although to be fair, I still have to Google how to boil an egg whereas my omelets and steak are on point. You see the secret to a perfectly prepared steak is to use a reverse sear method…but I digress.

Cover Cropping: Boiling an Egg

Feasibility: High

Why: Cover cropping is relatively simple to implement and doesn't require significant changes to existing farming practices. It's a straightforward way to improve soil health and reduce erosion, much like how boiling an egg is a basic cooking skill.

Example: Planting a rye cover crop during the off-season is easy and provides immediate benefits like weed suppression and soil fertility enhancement.

No-Till Farming: Frying an Omelet

Feasibility: Moderate

Why: No-till farming requires some investment in specialized equipment and a shift in farming routines. It's a bit more involved than cover cropping but still manageable with the right equipment, support and training, much like frying an omelet requires a bit more attention and technique than boiling an egg.

Example: Switching to a no-till seed drill can initially be a bit tricky, but once mastered, it offers significant benefits in soil structure and carbon sequestration. Although the jury is still out on the full benefits of total carbon sequestration as some studies have shown an increase in soil organic carbon (SOC) levels in the top 20cm, but a decrease in SOC below 20cm, leading to a net-neutral difference in the two techniques. I tend to fall on the side that no-till has several other benefits that far outweigh any mitigation of the overall SOC levels. One of these is the fact that tilled soil tends to decompose organic matter more quickly in the soil, leading to faster rates of CO_2 release. So even if net SOC levels were similar when accounting for deeper layers, the slower decomp rate afforded by no-till makes a positive impact for carbon sequestration. And the benefits to soil structure, water capacity and handling, soil biome and nutrient availability all more than make up for any other deficiencies.

Alternate Wetting and Drying (AWD): Grilling a Steak

Feasibility: Moderate to High

Why: AWD involves changes in water management practices, which can be implemented with existing irrigation systems. It requires careful monitoring but is less complex than agroforestry. Think of it as grilling a steak—requires attention to timing and temperature but is entirely doable with practice.

Example: Implementing AWD in rice paddies can be straightforward with proper training and support, leading to significant water savings and methane reductions.

Crop Rotation and Intercropping: Baking a Bread Loaf

Feasibility: Moderate

Why: Crop rotation and intercropping are more complex than they appear, much like baking a loaf of bread. While the concept might seem straightforward—swap out one crop for another—it requires a deep understanding of how crops interact with both the soil and each other. Farmers need to account for several factors, such as nutrient cycling, pest management, local climate, and market conditions. You don't want to plant a nutrient-draining crop immediately after another that depleted the same resources. This level of planning requires foresight and management to optimize short-term profits while maintaining long-term soil health.

In addition, the economics of each crop rotation decision must be carefully considered. For example, while rotating legumes with cereals improves soil fertility by fixing nitrogen, the timing of planting and market conditions for each crop have to be weighed. This process can be profitable in the long run but requires strategic thinking and thorough planning, much like a perfectly baked bread loaf—achievable but requiring precision and expertise. You don't want to be bringing your homemade pumpkin bread to market in July or your sourdough to market a month after all those TikTok influencers made everyone go out and get their own yeast starters.

Example: Rotating nitrogen-fixing legumes with nutrient-hungry cereals like wheat or maize improves soil fertility and reduces pest pressures. However, success hinges on understanding local soil conditions, pest dynamics, and crop marketability, which means the approach requires careful management and sometimes outside support to ensure effective crop cycles. Recent advances in AI and decision-support tools are helping farmers optimize these complex rotations, improving both yields and long-term soil health.

Agroforestry: Baking a Soufflé

Feasibility: Low to Moderate

Why: Agroforestry is much like baking a soufflé—complex, resource-intensive, and requiring a careful touch to achieve the desired result. It demands significant upfront investment in planning, tree species selection, and long-term maintenance. Like a soufflé, which can rise beautifully if handled with precision, agroforestry can yield tremendous benefits—enhanced biodiversity, carbon sequestration, and improved soil health—but the process must be approached with patience and expertise, and it isn't right for everyone. Not all crop systems are compatible with agroforestry; for example, it works well with coffee or certain silvopasture systems but may not suit large-scale monocrop farms. The costs and complexity of managing both trees and crops simultaneously make this practice a more specialized option, best suited to farms willing to make a long-term commitment.

Example: In agroforestry systems, trees are integrated into agricultural land to create a balanced ecosystem. For example, coffee farmers often plant shade trees, which not only improve biodiversity but also protect coffee plants from extreme weather conditions. However, this requires careful management of tree density and placement to prevent competition for resources like sunlight and water. Silvopasture systems, which combine forestry with livestock grazing, have great potential for carbon sequestration and sustainable land use. Though the rewards are high, the complexity and cost involved make agroforestry more like a well-executed soufflé: delicate, rewarding, and achievable only with careful attention to detail.

Future Technologies: What's Cooking on the Horizon?

As we look toward the future, the intersection of technology and sustainable farming promises exciting advancements, though not without its fair share of skepticism. Let's explore what's coming down the pipeline:

Optimistic Perspectives

Precision Agriculture Tools:

Advances in AI and IoT are making it easier for farmers to monitor and manage their fields with pinpoint accuracy. Drones and satellite imagery can provide real-time data on crop health, soil moisture, and pest infestations, allowing for more targeted interventions. Sensor systems being built into or added onto tractors, combines and other equipment allow for real-time decision-making and input prescriptions. It's like having a miniature agronomist riding on the edge of your applicator turning on and off the spigot as needed.

Blockchain-Based Traceability Systems:

Blockchain technology can revolutionize supply chain transparency, allowing consumers to trace their products back to their origins with ease. This not only builds trust but also ensures that sustainable practices are being upheld throughout the supply chain. It's like having a digital receipt that proves your apple was grown with love and care. At Spiro Carbon, we use blockchain technology to create a permanent, immutable record of all verification activity and the supporting data to go with it. This kind of transparent record keeping in multiple aspects of agriculture production adds confidence to the system and enables many new opportunities for consumer customization and its associated monetization.

Renewable Energy Integration:

Solar panels, wind turbines, and bioenergy systems are increasingly being integrated into farming operations, reducing reliance on fossil fuels and lowering operational costs. This is currently most effective further along the supply chain, like at packing and storage facilities, but use cases in the field are growing as the capabilities of small-scale renewable energy production improves. Imagine powering your tractor with the sun—put's a whole new meaning to "my big green tractor."

Biochar – Super Soil:

Biochar is a carbon-rich material created by heating organic biomass (think - agricultural waste) in a low-oxygen environment (a process called pyrolysis). Once applied to soil, biochar enhances soil structure, improves water retention, and boosts nutrient availability—all while sequestering carbon for centuries. Think of biochar as a "superfood" for soil, helping it retain moisture and nutrients while locking away carbon, which makes it an effective climate mitigation tool. Farmers could use biochar to rejuvenate degraded soils and improve crop yields, all while reducing their carbon footprint. This practice has the potential to transform agriculture, especially in regions with poor soil quality, by promoting sustainable farming and improving food security.

In practical terms, biochar can increase agricultural productivity by improving soil health, particularly in nutrient-poor or degraded soils. Its porous structure enhances water retention and nutrient availability, which can reduce the need for chemical fertilizers, saving costs and decreasing environmental harm. Additionally, biochar helps store carbon in the soil, contributing to long-term carbon sequestration—a critical benefit in the fight against climate change. The carbon captured during biochar production remains stable for hundreds, if not thousands, of years, locking it away from the atmosphere.

This makes biochar a win-win for both farmers and the environment, offering an innovative solution that could play a pivotal role in climate-smart agriculture. While the technology is still being refined for broader use, biochar holds immense promise as a tool for sustainable farming practices.

Skeptical Perspectives

High Costs and Accessibility:

While precision agriculture and blockchain systems offer significant benefits, their high initial costs and technological requirements can be prohibitive for smallholder farmers, especially in developing regions. It's like trying to buy a high-end espresso machine to take camping with your two-man tent.

Over-Hyped Technologies:

Not all new technologies live up to the hype. And in agriculture especially, the hype cycle is extremely difficult to traverse because it is very difficult to come back from that initial fall that inevitably comes with any newly hyped technology. Farmers tend to be conservative and once an innovation fails to deliver promised benefits, it leaves farmers disillusioned and financially strained and that initial impression is hard to overcome. Think of it as the soufflé that never rises—looks promising but falls flat when it counts.

Data Privacy and Security Concerns:

As farming becomes more digital, concerns about data privacy and security grow. Farmers may be wary of sharing sensitive information about their operations, fearing misuse or exploitation. It's the digital age equivalent of keeping your recipes under lock and key. In many cases, the farmers may not even know what to do with their data or understand how or why their data is of value, but they've been told that it is and so they become very protective of it. And let's face it, technology companies do not have a great track record of being good and fair stewards of their customers' data.

Balancing Optimism with Realism

While the technological advancements coming down the pipeline offer exciting opportunities, they should be approached with a healthy dose of realism. Technology holds transformative potential for sustainable agriculture, but we cannot assume a "one-size-fits-all" approach will work for every farmer or region. Let's break down the balance between optimism and the challenges:

Optimistic Perspectives: Technologies like precision agriculture, blockchain, and biochar show significant promise in making agriculture more sustainable and efficient. These innovations can optimize water use, improve yields, reduce chemical inputs, and enhance transparency in the supply chain. Take biochar, for example—its ability to enhance soil fertility while also sequestering carbon for the long term is a compelling solution for both productivity and climate action. Likewise, solar energy integration and other renewable energy sources could make farms more self-sufficient and eco-friendly, reducing operational costs over time.

Realistic Challenges: However, these advancements don't come without hurdles. Cost remains a significant barrier to adoption for smallholder farmers, especially in developing regions. Many of these technologies require substantial up-front investment, which can be difficult for farmers operating on thin margins. Accessibility is another issue, particularly when it comes to technical knowledge and training. Just as not every home cook can master a soufflé on the first try, not every farmer has the resources or skills to easily adopt these new techniques. Additionally, there are concerns about scalability: while some regions may benefit from precision tools or biochar, others may face limitations based on climate, soil type, or socioeconomic factors.

Then there's the risk of overhyping technologies. Just because something works well in a test environment or in the lab doesn't mean it's always practical on the ground. The agriculture industry is littered with the bodies of hyped technologies and products. Farmers have seen technologies come and go, and the risk-averse nature of agriculture means that many remain skeptical until results are consistently proven over time. If expectations aren't met, the backlash can be significant, slowing broader adoption.

Equitable Access and Support: For these innovations to truly take root, support systems need to be in place. Government subsidies, microfinancing, and education programs are essential to ensure that the benefits of these technologies reach all farmers, not just large-scale, tech-savvy ones. Without such support, we risk further deepening the digital and economic divide between wealthy and poor farmers, both within nations and globally. Additionally, concerns over data privacy and security are valid and must be addressed as more agricultural practices become data-driven. Farmers need clear, transparent agreements about how their data is used and how they can benefit from sharing it without fear of exploitation.

While the future of sustainable agriculture is filled with exciting possibilities, it's important to temper our expectations and acknowledge the challenges that come with it. Achieving widespread adoption will require not just innovative technology but also equitable access, practical training, and sustained support. When approached with balanced optimism and practical foresight, these advancements could transform global agriculture for the better.

Conclusion: Embracing the Green Path with Open Eyes and Ready Hands

Sustainable farming practices are the cornerstone of a resilient, productive, and environmentally friendly agricultural system. While the path to widespread adoption is fraught with challenges, understanding the different practices, overcoming barriers, and leveraging future technologies can pave the way for a greener future.

In the next chapter, we'll dive into the big money behind all this—how financial mechanisms like carbon markets, trade agreements, and corporate investments can fuel the transition to sustainable farming on a global scale. Spoiler alert: there's a lot of cash up for grabs, and the people who figure out how to tap into it will shape the future of agriculture. See you in Chapter 8!

8
Show Me the Money

So far, we've explored the technical and environmental benefits of sustainable farming. But let's get down to business—how do farmers, corporations, and entire economies monetize sustainable practices? In this chapter, we'll break down the different financial mechanisms available, critique the current system, and look at how these strategies can evolve to be more inclusive and equitable for all players involved, especially smallholder farmers.

Monetization Strategies: Cash for Carbon

Sustainable farming practices aren't just good for the planet; they can also be a money-maker—if you know where to look. Here are some of the main ways these practices can be monetized:

Carbon Credits: Compliance & Voluntary Markets

Carbon credits and carbon offsets are financial instruments used to reduce greenhouse gas (GHG) emissions. A carbon credit represents the right to emit one ton of carbon dioxide (or its equivalent in other GHGs). In compliance markets, governments set a cap on the total amount of GHGs that companies in certain industries can emit. Each company is allocated a specific limit (or cap) on emissions. If they emit less than their limit, they can sell their excess credits to other companies that have exceeded their limits. This creates a market-driven approach to emissions reductions, incentivizing businesses to reduce their carbon footprint.

A carbon offset, on the other hand, represents a reduction in emissions made elsewhere—such as planting trees or investing in renewable energy projects—that a company can purchase to "offset" its own emissions. Offsets are typically used in voluntary markets, but they can also be part of compliance systems if regulators allow companies to meet part of their emissions reductions through offsets.

Compliance Markets: These are formal carbon markets where large corporations and governments buy carbon credits to meet mandatory GHG reduction targets. Think of it as paying to cover your shortfall in emissions reductions (but only within limits). Companies in sectors like energy or aviation purchase these credits, which come from certified projects that reduce or sequester carbon, such as reforestation or methane capture on farms. The most common compliance markets include systems like the EU Emissions Trading System (EU ETS) and California's Cap-and-Trade Program but the list of compliance markets is growing as more national governments implement their own systems to spur the effort towards reaching their NDC. These markets are critical in regulating emissions in high-polluting industries and encouraging reductions through financial incentives. For industries where emissions are very high, it is unrealistic to expect an immediate switch to carbon neutrality. And for some industries, the idea of a truly carbon neutral state is unreachable given the current limits of technology. This is where the importance of compliance markets really shows. One feature of compliance markets is to encourage regulated companies to reduce their footprints internally by reducing the allowed emission levels each year, imposing a financial incentive through the forms of taxes and penalties if they don't. The good old stick approach.

Voluntary Offset Markets: In contrast to compliance markets, voluntary carbon markets cater to companies and individuals looking to voluntarily offset their carbon footprints. Farmers who implement practices like no-till farming or AWD (Alternate Wetting and Drying) can sell their carbon sequestration or methane reduction as credits to buyers in these markets. It's a smaller market but growing as more brands push for sustainability credentials to meet internal goals or respond to consumer demand. Unlike compliance markets, voluntary markets are less regulated, which has led to a number of issues, including accusations of greenwashing—the practice of companies overstating or misrepresenting their environmental actions.

Two major registries, Verra and Gold Standard, play a key role in certifying voluntary carbon projects. These organizations set the rules and frameworks that projects must follow to generate carbon credits, such as ensuring that emission reductions are real, additional (i.e., wouldn't have happened without the project), and permanent. However, despite these standards, some high-profile scandals have emerged.

For example, in early 2023, Verra was accused of issuing credits for forest conservation projects that had vastly overestimated the carbon savings, leading to claims that some credits were essentially worthless and did not represent real-world emission reductions. This controversy highlighted the lack of transparency and potential flaws in the voluntary carbon market, reinforcing the need for stronger regulation and verification to ensure integrity.

Verra, of course, strenuously disagreed and offered a rebuttal with their own scientific analysis. Regardless of the veracity of the claims on either side, it did enormous damage to the reputation of the industry as a whole and the voluntary market especially.

There are other major issues with the current state of both voluntary and compliance markets which we'll address in a little bit. In fact, these other issues are the entire reason we started Spiro Carbon in the first place. These challenges point to the ongoing need for vast improvements in how carbon markets operate to ensure that they truly drive meaningful climate action.

Pro Tip: The value of carbon credits varies widely, with compliance market credits fetching higher prices than most voluntary market ones. In 2022, carbon prices on compliance markets ranged from $40 to over $130 per ton of CO_2 equivalent (CO_2e), whereas, with a few exceptions, voluntary markets averaged between $5 and $20 per ton. In 2024, thanks to numerous scandals in the voluntary market and an overall wariness of companies to trust offsets to reach their goal, the price of voluntary offsets plummeted to as low as 25 cents per ton. You would have been better offer investing in Beanie Babies at that point. Most people in the industry agree that prices will rise and return to or exceed previous values but drastic changes must be implemented to regain the credibility and trust that was lost over the last two years in many of these projects.

Carbon Insetting

Insetting, like me with my extended family, is often considered the more effective, better-looking cousin of offsetting in the sustainability world. Rather than buying carbon credits from unrelated projects, insetting involves making direct investments within a company's own supply chain to reduce its Scope 3 emissions. This approach aligns emission reductions more closely with the company's core operations, making it more defensible and authentic compared to offsets from external projects. While the ultimate goal of both insetting and offsetting is to reduce global carbon footprints, insetting's focus on reducing emissions within a company's supply chain provides more directly tangible results.

Unlike offsetting, where companies might finance unrelated projects like reforestation efforts in distant locations, insetting creates measurable benefits within a company's own operations. For instance, if a chocolate company pays cacao farmers to adopt agroforestry practices—integrating trees with crops—it generates a carbon "inset." This reduction directly decreases the emissions related to the chocolate production process, making it a more transparent and strategic reduction within the company's Scope 3 (indirect) emissions.

The primary advantage of insetting lies in its authenticity. It's viewed as more credible than traditional carbon offsets because the emission reductions are a direct result of activities linked to the company's product, not a separate, unrelated project. As a result, insetting helps companies reduce their carbon footprint in real time rather than relying on external reductions, which might not directly correlate with their supply chain's impact. It's also easier to communicate these actions to stakeholders, given that they're tangible and traceable within the company's operations.

Insetting in the agricultural supply chain is particularly impactful. Many agricultural supply chains have large Scope 3 footprints due to farming activities, transportation, and raw material production. A company like Nestlé, for example, could pay coffee farmers to implement sustainable practices such as regenerative agriculture or no-till farming to sequester more carbon and reduce methane emissions. Or a fertilizer company could pay farmers whose nitrogen use efficiency increases due to the adoption of precision agriculture. This is when the yield to input ratio improves and directly affects the fertilizer producer's scope 3 emissions. These actions benefit the farmers directly, making their land more resilient to climate change, while also reducing the company's environmental impact.

By working within their own supply chains, companies can achieve multiple benefits through insetting, including:

- Stronger supplier relationships by supporting farmers and other supply chain partners.
- More resilient supply chains, since sustainable practices often result in higher yields and better soil health.
- A reduction in the company's overall carbon footprint that's more defensible and concrete, avoiding accusations of greenwashing.
- Improved optics for both investors and consumers, as insetting signals a genuine commitment to sustainability. The optics are key: while the net environmental benefit may be the same as offsetting, insetting is seen as a more proactive and credible solution because it demonstrates direct responsibility for emissions rather than outsourcing the solution.

Companies still need to pay for these changes to take place, just like they would for carbon credits or carbon offsets, but because the relationship is within their own supply chain with vendors whom they have already engaged in trade, there are no external markets for insets like there are for credits and offsets. But a lack of markets doesn't mean companies are totally on their own. Many GHG project developers and verification bodies can help facilitate the arrangement between a company and its suppliers to set up, manage, verify and quantify the insetting reduction. Insetting serves as a highly strategic method for companies to both meet sustainability goals and enhance their supply chains, all while presenting a clearer, more transparent method of reducing emissions in a way that aligns directly with their business operations.

Regulatory Benefits, Taxes & Tariffs

Government Incentives and Taxes play a crucial role in encouraging both companies and farmers to adopt more sustainable practices, often offering significant financial benefits for doing so. These incentives come in the form of tax credits, subsidies, tariffs, and other programs aimed at reducing greenhouse gas emissions and promoting environmental sustainability.

One prominent example is the *45Z Tax Credit* under the U.S. Inflation Reduction Act (IRA), which is aimed at ethanol producers and other biofuel manufacturers. The 45Z credit provides financial incentives to producers of clean fuels based on their carbon intensity (CI). The credit encourages ethanol producers to lower their carbon footprint by improving production processes, sourcing lower-carbon inputs, or adopting carbon capture technologies. The idea is to make biofuels more competitive with fossil fuels while also incentivizing further emissions reductions across the fuel supply chain.

Beyond the 45Z credit, many other programs exist that reward sustainable practices:

Carbon Border Adjustment Mechanism (CBAM): The EU's CBAM is a pioneering example of tariffs being linked to carbon emissions. Starting in 2026, companies exporting goods into the EU will face a tax or tariff based on the carbon footprint of their products. This policy aims to level the playing field for EU companies subject to carbon regulations and will incentivize foreign producers to adopt lower-emission methods to avoid additional fees. Currently, CBAM only applies to a handful of commodities, but it is expected to expand the scope of included goods in the future. Farmers who use sustainable practices, such as reduced emissions in fertilizer use or adopting carbon-sequestration techniques, may be able to help their buyers avoid or minimize these tariffs in the future, giving them a competitive edge in global markets. Likewise, other countries have jumped on the BAMwagon...see what I did there? They're looking at implementing their own tariffs on imports based on carbon footprints or at least requiring carbon accounting measures for many products.

Section 45Q Tax Credit: The U.S. offers tax credits for carbon capture, utilization, and storage (CCUS) projects under Section 45Q. This program encourages companies, including agricultural processors, to invest in technologies that capture CO_2 emissions and either store them underground or repurpose them for other industrial uses. This is particularly relevant to bioethanol or biodiesel producers who are exploring ways to reduce the carbon intensity of their products through CCUS.

Green Tariff Programs: In some countries, producers of sustainable agricultural products may benefit from reduced tariffs or preferential trade agreements. Countries that emphasize low-carbon agriculture or sustainable farming methods may negotiate these trade deals to incentivize other nations to adopt greener practices in exchange for tariff reductions or preferential market access.

Farm Bill Subsidies: In the U.S., the Farm Bill provides subsidies and financial assistance to farmers adopting conservation and sustainable practices. Programs like the Conservation Stewardship Program (CSP) and

Environmental Quality Incentives Program (EQIP) offer cost-sharing options for farmers who implement practices like no-till farming, cover cropping, or buffer zones to protect waterways. These subsidies help lower the financial burden of transitioning to more sustainable practices.

These programs and policies demonstrate how governments can encourage sustainable practices by lowering financial barriers for farmers and producers. They also show the growing trend of linking international trade and domestic policy to carbon intensity. As emissions regulations tighten, sustainable practices won't just be a nice-to-have; they'll be economically essential to avoid penalties like tariffs, while also providing access to valuable tax credits and subsidies.

By coupling sustainability with financial incentives, these policies drive industries toward lower emissions, positioning sustainable farming practices as both environmentally responsible and economically viable in the long term.

Payments for Ecosystem Services

Payments for Ecosystem Services (PES) reward farmers and landowners for the ecological benefits that their land management provides beyond traditional marketable goods like crops or livestock. These services, which include things like water purification, carbon sequestration, biodiversity support, and flood mitigation, are often undervalued because they don't have direct market prices. PES programs work by assigning a monetary value to these benefits, thus creating an incentive for farmers to adopt practices that improve environmental outcomes.

One of the key advantages of PES is that it aligns environmental protection with economic incentives, offering farmers a new revenue stream for adopting sustainable practices. PES programs are often implemented by governments, non-governmental organizations, or international institutions like the World Bank, which seeks to expand PES on a global scale to incentivize sustainable land use in developing regions.

Example: Costa Rica is a pioneering country in the implementation of PES. Its Payments for Environmental Services Program (Pagos por Servicios Ambientales) has been in place since the 1990s. This program compensates landowners for managing their land in ways that contribute to carbon sequestration, biodiversity conservation, water protection, and scenic beauty. The program is funded through a tax on fossil fuels and has been credited with helping Costa Rica achieve significant reforestation and environmental restoration.

Internationally, organizations like the World Bank are exploring large-scale PES systems to encourage sustainable land management in areas prone to deforestation or environmental degradation. By integrating PES into global initiatives, they aim to provide financial incentives for countries and communities to preserve forests, wetlands, and other ecosystems that serve as carbon sinks or biodiversity hotspots. The UN REDD+ Program is another example, where developing countries are paid to reduce emissions from deforestation and forest degradation.

While PES programs have shown success, they are not without challenges. These include ensuring fair and equitable access for smaller or more marginalized farmers, developing long-term funding mechanisms, and creating robust monitoring and verification systems to ensure that the environmental benefits are genuinely being delivered. Additionally, scaling PES to cover larger areas or more complex ecosystems can be administratively and technically challenging, requiring significant coordination across various sectors and levels of government.

PES schemes represent a promising way to reward

farmers and landowners for their contributions to environmental sustainability, transforming ecological stewardship into an economically viable pursuit. As interest in sustainability grows, the expansion of PES programs is likely to become a critical component in global efforts to combat climate change and protect natural ecosystems.

Premium Market Labels

Certifications like Organic, Fair Trade, and Rainforest Alliance allow farmers to sell their products at premium prices by tapping into environmentally conscious consumer markets. These certifications signal to buyers that the products have been grown with practices that emphasize sustainability, ethical labor, and biodiversity conservation. Similarly, organizations like the Sustainable Rice Platform (SRP) and the International Rice Research Institute (IRRI) offer marketing labels for rice grown under their certified sustainable programs, which focus on reducing water use, cutting methane emissions, and improving farmer livelihoods.

Farmers who adopt these sustainable practices gain access to high-value markets, where consumers are increasingly willing to pay more for eco-labeled products. Research indicates that consumer demand for sustainability has been growing, particularly in industries like food and beverage, textiles, and agriculture. This shift in consumer behavior boosts profits for farmers who invest in certifications, creating a direct financial incentive to maintain sustainable practices. For example, Fair Trade-certified farmers often receive a price premium above the market rate, while Rainforest Alliance-certified products command higher prices due to their association with environmental and social responsibility.

In addition to financial benefits, these certifications can also enhance brand reputation and market access for producers, especially in export markets where sustainability is increasingly a requirement rather than an option. This ecosystem of sustainable certifications and marketing labels plays a crucial role in making sustainable farming not just an ethical choice, but a profitable one as well.

Government Subsidies

Many governments provide subsidies and direct financial support to encourage farmers to transition to sustainable practices. In the U.S., the Department of Agriculture (USDA) offers financial assistance through initiatives like the Environmental Quality Incentives Program (EQIP), which helps cover the costs associated with sustainable practices such as cover cropping, no-till farming, and transitioning to organic methods. However, access to these funds can be inconsistent and dependent on annual budget allocations, meaning some farmers may struggle to secure support depending on location and fund availability.

Internationally, similar programs exist. For example, in Brazil, the government has implemented the Low-Carbon Agriculture Plan (ABC Plan), which offers subsidized loans to farmers who adopt sustainable agricultural practices like agroforestry, integrated crop-livestock systems, and improved pasture management. These loans are designed to reduce the environmental impact of farming in one of the world's largest agricultural exporters. The ABC Plan not only targets emission reductions but also seeks to enhance productivity and resilience in the agricultural sector, demonstrating a broader approach to sustainable development.

In New Zealand, the Sustainable Land Management and Climate Change (SLMACC) program supports farmers with research and grants to adopt sustainable practices and reduce the carbon footprint of farming. This program specifically helps farmers mitigate the impacts of climate change by encouraging the use of technologies and practices that reduce emissions and improve land management.

These examples show how governments across the globe are incentivizing sustainable farming practices. However, like the U.S., many of these programs face challenges with funding availability and accessibility, particularly for smallholder farmers. More robust and consistent funding mechanisms are needed to ensure broader adoption of sustainable practices.

There are also government-subsidized insurance programs in several countries that help cover crop or yield loss when implementing new sustainable practices for the first time. These programs aim to reduce the financial risk for farmers who transition to sustainable methods, ensuring that any potential short-term yield reductions are mitigated.

U.S. Federal Crop Insurance Program (FCIP): In the United States, the USDA's Risk Management Agency (RMA) offers crop insurance policies that are subsidized by the federal government. Farmers who adopt conservation practices like cover cropping or no-till farming can still be eligible for crop insurance, and in some cases, the USDA has provided specific premium discounts to farmers who implement these practices. For example, the Conservation Stewardship Program (CSP) offers insurance adjustments or credits for adopting sustainable land management practices. While the program doesn't exclusively cover yield losses from implementing new sustainable practices, it does provide financial incentives and risk management for farmers undergoing the transition.

Prevented Planting Coverage: As part of the U.S. crop insurance system, there are provisions like Prevented Planting Coverage, which offers insurance when a farmer cannot plant due to adverse weather or other conditions, including transitioning to conservation practices that may affect timing or yield in the short term.

Canadian AgriInsurance Program: In Canada, under AgriInsurance, provinces work with the federal government to provide coverage for crop losses due to natural disasters, including losses that may arise when farmers adopt sustainable practices like conservation tillage or organic farming. Though this program isn't exclusively for sustainable agriculture, it helps cover yield loss during transitions.

EU Common Agricultural Policy (CAP): In the European Union, there are also support mechanisms tied to the Common Agricultural Policy (CAP), which includes subsidies for crop insurance and financial protection when farmers adopt new agri-environmental schemes. Though direct insurance programs may not always be tied to specific sustainable practices, the CAP provides financial assistance to cover income loss or yield variability, often indirectly supporting farmers through environmental payments and risk management programs.

Mexico's CADENA Program: Mexico has the CADENA Program, which provides risk management tools for farmers, including insurance that covers losses due to natural disasters and climate variability. While not specifically designed for sustainable farming practices, CADENA offers risk coverage for smallholder farmers adopting new techniques in response to climate impacts, which can include sustainable practices.

These programs reflect how various governments aim to de-risk the transition to sustainable agriculture. Although there isn't always a specific insurance program solely for sustainable practices, many existing crop insurance systems accommodate or incentivize sustainability by offering coverage for yield losses or providing incentives like premium reductions. However, there is still room for growth in designing specific insurance products that fully address the unique risks tied to adopting sustainable farming practices.

Evaluating Effectiveness: The Rich Get Richer?

While these monetization strategies offer exciting opportunities, like most things in life, they often disproportionately benefit large, well-capitalized operations at the expense of smaller ones. Here's why:

The Big Farm Bias:

Larger farms have better access to the tools, expertise, and capital needed to meet certification standards, implement new technologies, or navigate carbon markets. For example, enrolling in a carbon credit program can require significant upfront investment in measurement, verification, and reporting—costs that smallholder farmers may struggle to bear. The registration process alone for one of the big registries is so onerous that project developers have no incentive to work with small farms as part of a larger project.

Exclusion of Smallholders:

Small farms, especially in the Global South, often lack the infrastructure to participate in carbon credit markets or earn PES payments. These markets frequently require standardized monitoring and auditing, which can be expensive. Without subsidies or support from NGOs or government bodies, many smallholder farmers are left out of these programs. When looking at who could benefit the most from them and who arguably is most impacted by the effects of climate change, it is ridiculous that the system, by its nature, excludes this group of participants.

The Downstream Effect:

Even when smaller farmers do participate, the benefits can be uneven. The costs of compliance and verification are often passed downstream to the farmer, and the added costs of sustainability may push up prices for consumers. In this sense, while these systems benefit corporations through lower emissions, they may not translate into direct gains for farmers—or consumers—in the short term. And total lack of transparency in almost every step of the process does nothing to improve this aspect of the inequality equation.

In short, while some people like to point to the many solutions being implemented by some of the larger companies in the space, both on the corporate agriculture supply chain side and on the climate solutions side, neither one seems to be doing a whole lot to address the massive inequality happening on the ground. And really, these smallholder farmers have been kicked around by larger interests for generations, so it's not like we should expect anything to change organically. Alright, it's soapbox time so hold on tight. In 2022, the aggregate total PROFIT for five of the world's top food companies, I'm not naming names, but you can do your own research, was around $41.77 Billion USD. They had average profit margins in the range of 10-15%. I understand they benefit from economies of scale and that they serve a vital role in the process. BUT… smallholder farmers in countries like Thailand face vastly different financial realities. Many smallholder farmers earn between $1,200 to $2,000 annually, depending on factors like crop yield, weather, and access to markets. This typically represents between 1% and 4% of the value of what they produce. In stark contrast, the top food companies not only capture a much larger share of the final sale price but also benefit from economies of scale and access to premium markets that smallholders are typically excluded from. This inequality underscores the challenges within the food supply chain, where the people producing raw materials receive only a fraction of the final value. Yeah, I get it. Big companies have big overhead, boo-freaking-hoo. This disparity is so significant because 1) while large food companies have the resources to capitalize on initiatives like carbon credits or premium product certifications, smallholder farmers—who often operate in challenging environments with less access to capital and technology—struggle to participate in these markets. And 2) there are very few pressures pushing bigger companies to do anything differently. A big reason for that is because so much of the attention is scattered and fragmented that consumers are easily distracted by small, disparate programs aimed at achieving maximum PR ROI rather than actual impact. Yes, I know I was the one advocating for the CEOs to support smallholder GHG projects earlier because they could get great PR out of it. I told you, I'm a capitalist and a realist. But for real impact to happen, we need to align the systems that affect profitability, driven by regulatory and consumer pressure with programs that address multiple sustainable development goals or issues. For the system to be more equitable, strategies such as tiered pricing, subsidized verification costs, or more accessible financial instruments are necessary to ensure that smaller operations can benefit from the same opportunities without being left behind. So, let's talk about some of those realistic solutions.

Proposed Solutions: Leveling the Playing Field

How can we make these monetization strategies work for everyone, not just the big players? Here are a few ideas:

Tiered Pricing Mechanisms

Implement a sliding scale for verification costs in carbon markets, where smaller farms pay lower fees relative to larger ones. This would reduce the financial burden on smallholders and make it easier for them to access these markets. This also works for applying a premium to "socially conscious" GHG reduction programs. Projects that promote social and economic justice in addition to their environmental benefits have a tangible value that is greater than those which do not. Consumers recognize this greater value, and research indicates that they will pay accordingly. The financial instruments, be they credits, offsets, insets or whatever, should have that premium pricing attached which can be passed on to the smallholder farmers and their local communities.

Simplified Verification Approaches

Aggregation models could allow small farms to bundle their sustainable practices and sell them as a group. Instead of each farm being individually verified for carbon credits, groups of farms could be evaluated together, reducing the per-farm cost of participation. This could be done through cooperatives or regional farm groups. This option has been proposed and while it seems fine on the face of it, it could lead to problems with fraud and overcounting like so many of the current scandal-ridden projects on the voluntary market.

Data Aggregation

A better solution is the recognition and adoption of more technology-driven MRV methods that allow for greater scaling down and cost efficiencies to provide low-cost, large-scale verification of sustainable practices, eliminating the need for expensive on-site inspections. Governments and NGOs could support these efforts to make them more accessible to smaller players. This is not a shameless plug, I promise, but it's a good example of what I'm talking about. At Spiro Carbon, our entire method for MRV is predicated on the idea of using low to no-cost remote data collection through satellites, a farmer mobile app, and other sources to be analyzed by artificial intelligence for accuracy, consistency and adherence to global standards. By automating this process, we remove the risk of human error and create a system that can scale up or down to any level, making it cost effective for projects of any size. By eliminating the friction of the cost and complexity of the verification process, you make it much easier for a wider range of potential projects to be included. Then by posting the results and all of the underlying data onto blockchain and making it available for the public to audit, you create a sense of radical transparency which engenders greater trust and credibility in the system.

Government and NGO Support

Governments should expand subsidies and grants for smallholder farmers to help cover the costs of transitioning to sustainable practices, but it's important to recognize that wealthier nations, which are committing funds to help smaller economies transition to greener methods, can allocate part of these financial resources toward directly supporting smallholder farmers. Even a small fraction of the billions pledged by developed countries for climate adaptation and mitigation could make a massive impact at the grassroots level. For example, if just 1% of the $100 billion annually committed by wealthier nations in climate financing were redirected toward subsidizing smallholder farmers, it would provide a significant boost to their ability to adopt sustainable practices. This would not only help reduce emissions and environmental degradation but also create more equitable growth by empowering the very people who are most vulnerable to the effects of climate change.

Similarly, large global funds like the Green Climate Fund (GCF) and other international climate finance mechanisms could work to make funding more accessible to smaller projects and smallholder farmers. While these funds tend to focus on large-scale projects, reallocating even a portion of the funds to target small, decentralized farming initiatives could have an outsized impact. The challenge, of course, lies in the administrative burden of providing oversight to a larger number of smaller projects. Tracking and verifying the effectiveness of hundreds or thousands of smaller-scale initiatives requires more infrastructure and resources for monitoring and reporting. However, this could be addressed by leveraging local NGOs, technology such as mobile apps, and satellite monitoring systems that reduce the cost and complexity of oversight while providing real-time feedback on project performance. Including a blockchain component in the reporting function would ensure greater transparency and could further reduce some of that administrative burden.

Involving smallholder farmers in global climate funds and subsidy programs would not only help to bridge the inequality gap but would also ensure that the most impacted communities can participate in and benefit from the transition to sustainable agriculture. By empowering these farmers, we create a win-win scenario where both global emissions are reduced, and local economies are strengthened. It's an investment with long-term environmental and socio-economic returns that wealthier nations, multilateral institutions, and global funds should prioritize.

Financial Impacts: From Farm to GDP

So, what happens if sustainable farming becomes the norm? Let's take a look at how it could impact the economy:

Farmer Income:

A shift to sustainable practices can increase farm profitability, especially if farmers access premium markets or sell carbon credits. In one study, organic farmers in the U.S. earned 22-35% more than conventional farmers due to higher premium prices for their produce.

Smallholder Impact: For smallholder farmers, participating in carbon insetting schemes or PES programs could increase income by up to 20%, providing a new, reliable revenue stream that reduces reliance on volatile commodity prices. Having a secondary source of income, not tied to the volatility of the physical commodity market, provides a huge improvement to the financial resiliency of an enormous group of people. This also has the potential to mitigate or reduce the strain on a country's resources to support these individuals when crops fail or catastrophe strikes.

National GDP:

In countries heavily reliant on agriculture, such as Vietnam or Ethiopia, large-scale adoption of sustainable farming could boost national GDP by increasing farm productivity, creating new green jobs, and reducing the economic impacts of climate-related crop failures. One study estimated that regenerative agriculture could increase GDP by 1-3% in low-income agricultural economies through improved yields and resilience.

Global Markets:

At the macro level, the rise of carbon trading and premium market labels could inject billions into global agricultural markets. The global carbon credit market alone is expected to reach $50 billion by 2030, driven by corporate demand for sustainable practices. As countries tighten environmental regulations, the demand for sustainable produce will only grow—potentially transforming entire supply chains.

Conclusion: The Green Dollar

While sustainable farming holds immense potential for monetization, current systems are skewed in favor of larger players. But with the right adjustments—tiered pricing, better verification systems, and more inclusive policies—we can ensure that smallholder farmers reap the benefits, too. The adoption of sustainable practices isn't just a win for the planet; it's also an opportunity for a more equitable and prosperous agricultural future.

9
Prove It

Meet Pablo, a smallholder farmer in the Andes, just trying to do the right thing. He's heard all about this carbon credit program and thinks, "Great! I'm already implementing sustainable farming practices, so this should be an easy win." Fast forward to him sitting at his kitchen table, staring down a Machu Picchu sized pile of paperwork. He's trying to figure out how to document the exact amount of carbon sequestered by the trees on his farm, how much water he's saved by implementing no-till farming, and why he needs a satellite image to prove his cows aren't producing as much methane as his neighbor's.

Pablo's experience highlights the struggle farmers face with Monitoring, Reporting, and Verification (MRV)—a critical but often overwhelmingly complex part of making sustainable farming practices financially viable.

The Importance of MRV

MRV, which stands for monitoring, reporting, and verification, is the backbone of sustainability projects. It's what gives carbon credits, sustainable certifications, and insetting projects their credibility. Without MRV, the entire system falls apart—there's no way to know if these projects are actually making a positive environmental impact or if they're just clever (or sometimes not-so-clever) accounting tricks. Unfortunately, as Pablo found out, MRV can feel more like filling out tax forms in a foreign language than saving the planet.

Farmers, especially smallholders, often face insurmountable hurdles trying to comply with MRV requirements. They might need to document everything from soil organic carbon levels to methane emissions, water usage, or even biodiversity changes. Even worse, the costs of MRV are typically passed down to the farmer. You want to play the carbon credit game? That'll be a few thousand dollars up front for data collection and verification.

Certainly, some of the giants in the agriculture space are offering easier programs for farmers to participate in by having them sign up, submit reports and get paid. But often times the accuracy of the reductions in these cases is questionable at best, leading one to wonder just how sustainable the program actually is and when the proverbial rug will get pulled. Also, the amounts farmers get paid in this manner are generally far less than the value of the credits they are producing, a familiar concept in the dynamic between farmer and buyer.

Current State of MRV: A Forest-Centric World

In the carbon market, GHG reduction programs are dominated by large-scale forest projects. These types of projects, like reforestation or avoided deforestation, are easier to monitor (relatively speaking) and can generate a ton of carbon credits in one fell swoop. Actually, they generate a whole bunch of tons of carbon credits and that's the point. A single forest project can encompass thousands or tens of thousands of hectares, which means the returns on MRV investment are much higher than in smaller, decentralized agricultural projects. In the MRV world, the saying goes: "gimme the big stuff and get outta here with that weak sauce". In all fairness, I've never actually heard another MRV company say that but that's what I imaging them saying when brought a project with a couple dozen smallholder farms.

Organizations like Verra and Gold Standard certify these projects, but their processes are tailored to large-scale, centralized efforts. These systems rely on satellite imagery, ground-based measurements, and a heavy dose of complex paperwork, which is challenging for large projects but almost impossible for smallholder farmers like Pablo to handle.

This leaves us with a system where most of the carbon credits traded in voluntary markets come from forestry projects, while agricultural projects, especially those implemented by smallholders, are left behind. It's no wonder why the majority of projects in developing countries are massive forest initiatives—they're easier to track, easier to verify, and generate much more revenue.

Here's the problem with that. I'm all for protecting the forests. I love trees. I spent most of my youth out in the woods and I have a deep appreciation for forest conservation projects and organizations. However, there are so many problems with relying on forest conservation as the main driver for carbon credit programs. Here's the thing: forest conservation projects, while noble and valuable, come with a ton of challenges when they are used as the primary mechanism for carbon credits. Let's break down some of the key issues.

First, conservation is like trying to prove a negative. If your project claims to have "avoided deforestation," how do you show that the trees would have been cut down without the project? You can't just claim that leaving things as they are has automatically resulted in avoided carbon emissions without solid evidence that deforestation was actually likely to happen. It's not easy to prove that something didn't happen just because the landscape remained intact. This is especially hard when there is little to no history of deforestation in a given area. It leads to murky validation practices where the line between what is real and what is speculative can get blurred. It's like me trying to get credit with my wife for not spending thousands of dollars on new tractor attachments I don't need. See how much money we saved? I should be rewarded for not spending money that I may or may not have been planning on spending anyway.

Next, afforestation and reforestation projects tend to focus on planting the cheapest trees possible to maximize financial gain. Often, this means planting fast-growing, non-native, or even monoculture species like eucalyptus or pine, which may not be suited to the local biome. These trees might soak up carbon, but they can also create environmental problems. For example, monoculture forests reduce biodiversity, can deplete local water resources, and are more susceptible to diseases and pests. Even native trees, if selected solely for their cost efficiency, can throw off the balance of an ecosystem that depends on a broader diversity of plant species.

Then there's the frontloading issue. Forest-based carbon credits often pay upfront based on the promise that the trees planted will continue to sequester carbon for decades—sometimes as long as 30 or 40 years. But what happens if those trees don't survive? Fires, pests, droughts, or illegal logging can wipe out an entire forest in a matter of days. If the trees are lost, the carbon credits tied to those trees become essentially worthless. Who bears that loss? Can the buyer of those credits ask for a refund? What kind of insurance exists to cover this? These risks make forest-based credits more volatile and raise questions about their long-term reliability.

Finally, let's not forget that large-scale forest projects often operate in regions where land tenure is unclear or contested. This can lead to land grabbing, displacement of local communities, or conflicts over land rights, particularly in developing countries. There are numerous reports of projects claiming land that local indigenous populations have relied on for generations, further complicating the ethical dimensions of these initiatives.

So, while forest conservation and afforestation are important for global carbon sequestration, they come with a host of challenges—both practical and ethical. Relying too heavily on them as the backbone of the carbon credit system ignores the complexity of ensuring real, long-term benefits for the environment and the communities involved. It also leaves out other, equally valuable sectors like agriculture, which could provide more verifiable and sustainable carbon reductions. But the MRV world and project developers love these projects because they are so data efficient. That causes a big problem since these are the main bodies driving the types of projects being initiated.

Data and Verification Issues: The Developing World Dilemma

Here's the rub: collecting accurate, timely data is hard. In developing countries, where infrastructure might be limited and farmers are often working with less formalized tools, gathering the data needed for MRV is even more difficult. Imagine trying to measure methane emissions from cows when you don't have access to sophisticated measuring devices—or even a reliable internet connection to submit the data. Good luck getting that approved by one of the major registries.

And then there's the cost. A smallholder farmer in Southeast Asia, for example, might be managing a few hectares of land. It's not economically feasible for them to pay thousands of dollars to measure soil carbon levels with any real precision. These are farmers who are already operating on razor-thin margins, and the additional burden of MRV makes participation in the carbon credit market practically impossible.

But there's hope—technology is starting to address these challenges. Satellite imagery, once the domain of governments and the very wealthy, is becoming more accessible. Drones, IoT sensors, and mobile apps are beginning to enable low-cost, decentralized data collection. Spiro Carbon (this time it is a shameless plug) is part of the wave of companies working to bring high-tech MRV solutions to smallholder farmers, using satellite data and AI-powered tools to automate the collection and analysis process. But even with these advances, there's still a gap in infrastructure, accessibility and especially finance that needs to be bridged.

Incentive Alignment: Making MRV Work for Everyone

At the heart of the issue is misaligned incentives. In theory, MRV is supposed to ensure that projects are credible and make a real impact. But in practice, it's often a cumbersome process that excludes the very people who could benefit the most from these programs—smallholder farmers.

We need to rethink how incentives are structured. Right now, the financial burden of MRV falls on the project developer or sponsor. This means the developer is going to choose those projects where his/her costs are lowest, and returns are highest. Agriculture offers some really high returns when viewed on a per hectare recurring basis. But for most, only well capitalized farms can afford to make the necessary changes, which discourages participation, and means project developers would have to shoulder that burden for small farms. That isn't likely to happen. One potential solution is to shift some of the cost to the buyers—after all, they're the ones ultimately benefiting from the carbon credits or sustainable certifications. Governments and NGOs could also play a role by subsidizing MRV for smaller projects or offering technical assistance.

Green Bonds represent a promising way to finance the transition to sustainable practices for smallholder farmers, offering a win-win scenario for investors seeking both financial returns and positive environmental impacts. By channeling investment into projects that help reduce greenhouse gas emissions, enhance biodiversity, or promote sustainable farming, these bonds can provide the capital necessary for smallholders to implement environmentally friendly practices without bearing the full financial burden upfront.

One innovative approach to making Green Bonds more attractive for both investors and smallholder farmers is coupling them with tax incentives. Tax incentives—such as deductions, credits, or exemptions—can entice investors by offering them additional financial benefits beyond the bond's yield, enhancing the appeal of these instruments. This would make Green Bonds a more viable option for raising the significant capital needed for sustainable agriculture projects.

Additionally, the use of carbon credits to guarantee the bond could further reduce financial exposure. Here's how it could work: as smallholder farmers adopt sustainable practices like no-till farming, agroforestry, or AWD, they generate carbon credits by reducing emissions or sequestering carbon. A portion of these credits could be pledged as collateral or a guarantee against the bond, providing bondholders with a tangible asset that mitigates risk. This model ties the financing directly to the environmental impact, ensuring that the projects not only generate financial returns but also verifiable ecological benefits. The use of blockchain for publicly reporting the verification of the sustainable activity means a higher degree of confidence that the bonds had the intended effect.

However, non-traditional financial instruments like Green Bonds for smallholders face challenges, particularly around credibility and scale. To make this model viable, it needs well-regarded champions—such as multilateral institutions, development banks, or high-profile corporations—that can provide trust, legitimacy, and technical support. Unfortunately, neither the institutional nor the retail investors of the world will just take this humble author's word for it. Entities like the World Bank or IFC could play a key role in underwriting or guaranteeing these bonds, making them more attractive to institutional investors. At the same time, these organizations could offer monitoring and verification services to ensure that the promised environmental benefits, such as carbon credits, are being delivered. If only we knew of a really great MRV company already set up to scale this transparently…ok, that was the last plug, I promise.

Furthermore, partnerships between private companies, governments, and NGOs would be essential in creating robust frameworks for these bonds. They could help streamline the issuance, distribution, and management of Green Bonds, and ensure that smallholder farmers have access to the necessary infrastructure, training, and market linkages to succeed.

By leveraging Green Bonds with tax incentives and carbon credit guarantees, this approach could unlock vast amounts of capital for the sustainable transition of smallholder farmers. Still, it requires strong partnerships and commitment from both the public and private sectors to realize its full potential.

Additionally, we need to make MRV more scalable and affordable. By embracing remote data collection methods like satellites, mobile apps, and automated AI verification systems, we can reduce the cost of MRV and make it accessible to more farmers, especially in developing countries. Programs that pool smallholder projects together to share the cost of MRV or providing developers with additional subsidies, tax breaks or other assistance to support these types of projects initially could also help level the playing field.

The future of MRV doesn't have to involve reams of paperwork and endless fees. With the right technology and incentive structure, we can create a system where Pablo and farmers like him can focus less on documentation and more on what they do best—farming sustainably.

10
But, But, But...

So, you've just made a pretty solid case for how sustainable farming practices, carbon markets, and innovative financing can help solve some of the biggest challenges facing agriculture and the climate today. But what about the critics? You know they're out there—questioning everything from the efficacy of carbon credits to the idea of paying farmers to adopt sustainable practices. In this chapter, we're diving into the naysayers' objections, addressing them head-on with data, common sense and a blind commitment to our point of view regardless of the... oh wait, never mind. Let's just get into it.

Addressing Criticisms: Why Carbon Markets and Monetization Schemes Aren't a Scam

To start with, this chapter is not to help refute people who don't believe in climate change. They require a different book. One with more pictures and smaller words. This is meant to address the criticisms of the mechanisms in place currently; those intended to help fix, mitigate or even reverse the effects of climate change. The most common criticism of carbon markets and monetization schemes in general is that they're just smoke and mirrors. People argue that carbon credits are just a way for big companies to greenwash their operations without making real changes. And sure, there are definitely some bad apples in the carbon market (remember those bogus forest credits?), but let's not throw out the whole bunch.

Refuting the Argument: Yes, the carbon market has seen its fair share of issues—additionality, leakage, and even outright fraud—but dismissing it entirely ignores the tremendous good it's done. After all, the EU ETS has driven a 43% reduction in emissions across major industries between 2005 and 2019, and similar programs worldwide are proving that we don't have the luxury of waiting for the perfect solution[27]. This is real, measurable progress.

Carbon Credits: This scheme has often been compared to the old tradition in the Catholic church of selling indulgences. Sinning was ok if you could afford to go and buy yourself clean. And look, I get it. On the face of it, that is what it appears to be. But in reality, for many industries, there is no way to feasibly hit the carbon neutrality goals required through internal measures in time relying on existing technologies and methods. By reallocating some of their capital, which I should point out could otherwise be going into other capital improvements or dividends and thus driving up the value of their stock, they are doing what is realistically feasible right now to make an impact. The atmosphere doesn't care whether that sequestered ton of CO_2 came from a reduction in your factory or the rice field down the road. It's all the same gas to them. And anyway, many carbon markets—particularly compliance markets—cap the amount of carbon credits a company can purchase, forcing them to make internal reductions first. The goal isn't just offsetting emissions but encouraging real, systemic change.

Case Study: In New Zealand, the Emissions Trading Scheme (ETS) has played a significant role in reducing deforestation. Between 2008 and 2018, deforestation rates dropped by 83%, largely due to the economic incentives provided by the scheme[28]. By monetizing carbon reductions, these programs incentivize companies and landowners to make decisions that benefit the environment, proving that it's not all about accounting gimmicks.

Insets: One argument against insetting is that it's often seen as "just another form of greenwashing." Skeptics argue that companies use insets to claim environmental responsibility while continuing harmful practices elsewhere, since insetting primarily involves internal supply chains rather than addressing broader systemic changes. These skeptics are jerks.

Refuting the Argument: Unlike offsets, where companies purchase credits from external projects, insetting encourages actual changes within a company's supply chain. This provides a more credible path toward sustainability since the company is taking direct responsibility for reducing its carbon footprint. Insetting requires the company to align its entire value chain with sustainability goals, making it harder to fake progress or ignore internal inefficiencies.

Additionally, by improving the sustainability of its supply chain, a company can increase resilience, enhance long-term profitability, and create more meaningful impact. Since it's linked to Scope 3 emissions, insetting has a direct relationship to the company's actual business activities— something that external offsets can't claim as readily.

Case Study: Nespresso has been a major proponent of insetting. Through its AAA Sustainable Quality™ Program, the company works directly with coffee farmers to implement agroforestry practices and improve soil management. Not only does this reduce the carbon footprint of Nespresso's coffee production, but it also improves farmers' yields and incomes[29]. This is a clear case of how insetting can deliver measurable environmental and social benefits within a company's supply chain, not just as a PR move.

Carbon Project Shortcomings: Critics often bring up the issue of additionality, arguing that some carbon credits come from projects that would have happened anyway. But good MRV practices ensure that carbon reductions are truly 'additional'—i.e., they wouldn't have happened without the project in place. Likewise, concerns about leakage and double-counting can be mitigated through rigorous tracking and transparency, which are already being addressed in newer iterations of carbon markets.

Terms Defined

Additionality: The concept that some carbon credits represent reductions that would have happened anyway, even without the project being implemented.

Leakage: When emissions reductions in one area lead to increased emissions elsewhere.

Double Counting: When two parties claim the same carbon reduction in different markets.

One of the most common critiques of carbon markets is the perceived lack of integrity. Critics often cite issues like greenwashing, additionality, and leakage, arguing that the system allows for more "fudging" than actual emissions reduction. These criticisms, while valid in some cases, are largely the result of outdated verification systems that have struggled to keep up with the rapid expansion of global carbon markets. But here's the good news: technology is quickly changing the game, and so are evolving regulatory frameworks.

Take blockchain technology, for example. Originally designed for financial transactions, blockchain is now being applied to carbon markets to ensure transparency and reduce fraud. The immutable nature of blockchain allows for a secure, verifiable, and tamper-proof record of transactions and carbon credit ownership. It ensures that once a credit is sold, it can't be double-counted in another market, tackling one of the major issues with voluntary carbon markets today—double counting. When combined with smart contracts, blockchain can also automate compliance, only releasing payments once all MRV conditions have been met and verified.

Additionally, AI-powered remote sensing and satellite monitoring have been game-changers for MRV. These technologies can monitor large tracts of land with a level of precision and frequency that was previously unimaginable. For example, AI can analyze satellite data to track changes in land use or forest cover, helping to verify whether reforestation projects are genuinely delivering the carbon sequestration they promised. Drones and IoT sensors are also playing a role, particularly in agricultural projects, where they can provide real-time data on soil health, methane emissions, or water use, ensuring that sustainability claims are backed by hard evidence although the cost of these data collectors can be prohibitive for many project types.

These advancements don't just address issues of fraud—they also make carbon markets more accessible to smaller players like smallholder farmers, who previously couldn't afford the high costs of traditional verification methods. As more projects integrate these technologies, the accuracy and integrity of carbon credits will continue to improve, making it harder for companies to greenwash their emissions reductions.

Furthermore, evolving regulatory frameworks are

stepping up to ensure market integrity. Take the Taskforce on Scaling Voluntary Carbon Markets (TSVCM), for example. Launched in 2020, this initiative aims to establish a set of global standards for carbon credits, making it easier to assess their quality and validity across markets. This effort seeks to weed out low-quality or fraudulent credits, ensuring that the entire market operates with greater transparency and accountability. Similarly, regulatory bodies like the International Carbon Reduction and Offset Alliance (ICROA) are working to refine standards that govern project eligibility, verification processes, and credit issuance.

While these systems are not perfect, they represent significant progress. By leveraging cutting-edge technology and stronger regulation, carbon markets are becoming more credible, which in turn encourages more companies to adopt genuine carbon-reduction strategies rather than relying on loopholes or creative accounting to meet sustainability goals.

Tax Incentives and Regulatory Measures: Some critics argue that tax incentives and regulatory measures like carbon taxes or credits are either too lenient or overly burdensome. They claim that the financial benefits go mostly to large corporations that can afford to make the changes, leaving small players behind. There's also concern that these measures are often complex and inconsistently applied across sectors, leading to loopholes and inefficiencies. Full disclosure, I'm one of these critics. But I recognize the value of this as a tool if/when applied correctly, consistently and fairly.

Refuting the Argument: While it's true that tax incentives often disproportionately benefit large corporations, it's not a reason to dismiss them entirely. In fact, the whole point of these incentives is to make sustainability profitable—if corporations are using them, that's a sign they're working. However, governments should refine these policies to ensure that smaller businesses also benefit. This could include simplifying the application process for tax credits, offering tiered incentives based on company size, or directly funding smaller projects.

Additionally, well-designed tax systems, like the EU's Carbon Border Adjustment Mechanism (CBAM), ensure that regulation is applied fairly. CBAM, for example, imposes tariffs on carbon-intensive imports, leveling the playing field for domestic companies that already adhere to strict carbon reduction regulations. These kinds of measures can help shift entire industries toward greener practices without unfairly penalizing the domestic economy. There are a lot of people who are not happy about CBAM. Most of these people will have to pay more to import goods into the EU because of it. And there is some economic justification for showing why it is not all sunshine and unicorn sprinkles, especially when looking at the impact on consumer pricing. But we can't have our Volvos and eat them, too. Or something like that. We've ridden the gravy train of cheap production at the expense of the environment for a long time and at some point, prices will go up, margins will shrink, and the world will have to adjust. The alternative is much worse.

Case Study: The 45Q tax credit in the U.S. is an example of how tax policy can drive large-scale carbon capture and storage (CCS) projects. By offering a tax credit of up to $50 per ton of CO_2 captured, the program incentivizes companies to adopt carbon capture technologies. One standout project is the Petra Nova facility in Texas, which captured over 1 million tons of CO^2 per year before being suspended (due to economic conditions, not technical failure). While large corporations primarily use these incentives, their impact is undeniable—without 45Q, CCS projects would not be economically viable.

Regulatory Schemes: The primary criticism of regulatory schemes like carbon taxes or cap-and-trade systems is that they disproportionately affect high-emitting industries, causing economic strain without necessarily delivering enough environmental benefit. Critics also argue that these systems sometimes allow wealthier companies to simply "buy their way out" of emissions reduction obligations, especially when credits can be traded freely.

Refuting the Argument: Cap-and-trade and carbon tax systems create powerful incentives for innovation. When industries face financial penalties for emitting GHGs, they're forced to innovate and find ways to reduce emissions—whether through energy efficiency, renewable energy, or other low-carbon technologies. These systems are designed to drive emissions reductions by making it more expensive to pollute, ultimately leading to the transformation of high-emitting sectors.

Yes, companies can buy carbon credits, but most cap-and-trade systems place a limit on how many credits companies can buy before they are required to make internal reductions. Additionally, the gradual tightening of caps ensures that emissions limits get stricter over time, pushing companies to take more aggressive action.

Case Study: The British Columbia Carbon Tax is one of the most successful examples of how carbon taxes can work. Since its introduction in 2008, the tax has helped reduce per capita fuel use by 19%, while GDP growth in the province has outpaced the rest of Canada. This dispels the myth that carbon taxes hinder economic growth. Instead, they promote both environmental and economic resilience.

The Climate Purist Dilemma: The Strawman Argument

Ah, climate purists. You know the type—those who argue that unless a solution is 100% perfect, we should do nothing at all. Waiting for the silver bullet, the climate purists often dismiss real-world solutions as "too little, too late." You can never please these folks. Ricky Nelson had a great song that speaks to this. No, I'm not quite old enough to remember when he was top of the charts, but my dad was a fan and Garden Party was one of my favorites. His advice that "You can't please everyone, so you've got to please yourself" is pretty solid when it comes to dealing with climate purists.

Let's paint an exaggerated picture. Meet "Gregory Purist," who insists that unless we implement a solution that completely eliminates all GHG emissions, promotes biodiversity, provides income for all smallholder farmers, and makes unicorns fly, it's not worth doing. Gregory's motto: "Perfection or nothing."

Here's the thing—Gregory's idea sounds noble, but it's also completely unrealistic. To begin with, if a unicorn could fly, it would technically be a Pegasus and then it would have to be classified as genetically modified which would make an entirely different group of critics angry. But mythical equines aside, waiting for the perfect solution is like waiting for a meteorologist to give you a 100% accurate weather forecast for next year's Fourth of July picnic. Instead of holding out for the perfect, we need to embrace the good, the practical, and the achievable.

Climate purists often say carbon markets don't do nearly enough. Well, guess what? We know that. You're not providing new information. But…it's better to have an imperfect system that prevents 1 gigaton of CO_2 from entering the atmosphere right now than to wait for Gregory's magic wand that will never come. For a species that thrives on instant gratification, you'd think we'd be more inclined to seek immediate results than wait for optimal outcomes. Regardless, the longer we wait, the more expensive the solution will become.

Refuting the Strawman: In reality, every ton of CO_2 kept out of the atmosphere matters. Carbon markets, imperfect though they may be, have the potential to reduce emissions significantly in the short term. Take California's cap-and-trade program, which has been operational since 2013 and has helped the state meet its 2020 GHG reduction goals four years early. It is far from perfect and still has a long way to go. But waiting for a flawless system would have meant four more years of maximum emissions. To put that in perspective, that helped the state avoid emitting approximately 252 million metric tons of CO2 equivalent (MMTCO2e) over the four years that it reached its greenhouse gas (GHG) reduction goals ahead of the 2020 deadline. Or, in terms the rest of us can understand, it was the equivalent of taking 54.8 million cars off the road for a year. Not bad for not being perfect, huh Greg?

Making the Case for Practical Solutions: Don't Let Perfect Be the Enemy of Good

For companies worried about profitability, sustainable practices aren't just a cost—they're an investment. Studies show that companies with strong environmental credentials see higher long-term returns and improved brand loyalty. You don't have to be a climate activist to realize that going green is just good business.At the heart of the debate is a key question: Do we wait for the ideal solution, or do we work with what we have while constantly improving?

The answer is clear—we need to act now with the best available solutions and improve them as we go. Sustainable farming incentives, carbon credits, and green bonds might not solve every problem immediately, but they are real-world tools that can drive change. And we need to learn from the mistakes of the past. Looking back at the near miracle of the first Green Revolution and the work pioneered by Dr. Bourlaug, one possible answer to the criticism of where that approach has landed us ecologically, is that we took the solution and did not improve upon it sufficiently with a holistic view to what that meant beyond the immediate goal of higher yield. We must not make the same mistake with this environmental problem by focusing so narrowly on its perfection to the exclusion of the social, economic and other impacts our programs and solutions might bring.

Practical Case Studies:

1. *Methane Emissions Reduction in Rice Farming*: In the Philippines, the use of Alternate Wetting and Drying (AWD) has reduced methane emissions from rice paddies by up to 48%. Is AWD a perfect solution that solves every environmental issue in rice farming? No. There are still issues with N2O emissions. AWD alone does not address the problem of crop residue burning and PM2.5 release after harvest. But it is a highly effective practice, relatively easily and inexpensively implemented, that cuts emissions while improving water efficiency. And it can be scaled quickly to millions of hectares, creating the potential for tens of millions of tons of CO_2 savings every year.

2. *Brazil's Low-Carbon Agriculture (ABC) Plan*: Brazil's ABC Plan encourages sustainable farming practices like no-till and agroforestry by offering low-interest loans. Since its inception, the program has helped reduce millions of tons of CO_2 emissions. While it doesn't solve all the deforestation issues in the Amazon, it has had a positive impact on carbon reduction in Brazil's agricultural sector.

What we need are practical solutions that work in the short and medium terms. These programs can be tweaked and improved over time, but the idea is to get started now. We can't afford to wait for perfection.

The Big Picture: Progress, Not Perfection

Here's the truth—there's no single solution to climate change, food insecurity, or income inequality for smallholder farmers. It's going to take a combination of approaches—carbon markets, sustainable farming incentives, government subsidies, and private investment—all working together to get the job done.

And lest you think the only motivation for this is saving the world and the yellow spotted jackalwhompus, there is a business case to made as well. For companies worried about profitability, sustainable practices aren't just a cost—they're an investment. Studies show that companies with strong environmental credentials see higher long-term returns and improved brand loyalty. You don't have to be a climate activist to realize that going green is just good business. The idea that sustainable practices are just an additional cost is increasingly outdated. In fact, adopting sustainability as part of a company's core operations can drive significant long-term returns, enhance brand reputation, and improve risk management. Let's dive into some verifiable data to back this up:

Sustainability Enhances Financial Performance (no pills required)

Multiple studies have shown that companies that embrace sustainable practices perform better financially over the long term. According to a report by Oxford University and Arabesque Partners, businesses that adopt environmental, social, and governance (ESG) standards tend to outperform those that do not, with 88% of the reviewed studies showing better operational performance, and 80% showing better stock price performance[30].

Sustainable Companies Attract Consumers

Consumers increasingly demand sustainable products, and they're willing to pay a premium for them. A Nielsen report found that 73% of global consumers are willing to change their consumption habits to reduce environmental impact, and 41% are willing to pay more for products that come from companies committed to sustainability[31].

Lower Operating Costs and Higher Efficiency

Sustainable practices often lead to lower operating costs. For example, energy efficiency measures can reduce utility bills, and waste reduction initiatives can lower material costs. Research from McKinsey & Company shows that reducing greenhouse gas emissions not only helps the environment but can also cut operating costs by as much as 10-20% in some sectors[32]. For example, General Motors saved $2.4 million annually by reducing energy use at its plants, and Walmart saved more than $100 million in a single year by reducing packaging waste and improving its supply chain efficiency.

Reduced Risk and Improved Regulatory Compliance

Sustainability also helps mitigate risks, particularly in industries vulnerable to climate regulations. Companies that reduce their environmental impact are better positioned to comply with future regulations, such as carbon taxes or stricter environmental laws. Not addressing sustainability early can expose companies to significant regulatory risk and brand damage[33]. This is just common sense and there are dozens of examples of this being successfully implemented for other sectors over the past century.

Investors are Prioritizing ESG

The financial industry is rapidly embracing sustainability. According to Bloomberg, ESG assets are on track to exceed $50 trillion by 2025, representing over one-third of total global assets under management. Investors are favoring companies with strong sustainability credentials because they are seen as less risky and more likely to be successful in the long term[34].

Here is a list of more recent examples of this playing

out in the real world. Granted, there are many factors that go into a company's valuation, revenue and growth, but it is hard to make an argument these companies were hurt by their implementation of sustainability activities.

Microsoft: In 2020, Microsoft made headlines by committing to become carbon negative by 2030. This means they aim to remove more carbon than they emit. By 2050, Microsoft plans to remove all the carbon the company has emitted directly or by electrical consumption since it was founded in 1975. In 2021, Microsoft revealed that it had already reduced its Scope 1 and 2 emissions by 17%. This massive sustainability commitment hasn't hurt its profitability—in fact, Microsoft's stock has risen by over 50% since their carbon-negative announcement[35][36].

Unilever: Unilever doubled down on its sustainability strategy during the pandemic, pledging to reach net-zero emissions from its products by 2039 and committing €1 billion to a new climate and nature fund. Even amid the pandemic-induced economic turbulence, Unilever reported a 9.2% increase in underlying sales growth in 2021 and attributed much of this success to its portfolio of "sustainable living" brands, which now make up 75% of the company's total sales. Brands like Hellmann's and Ben & Jerry's, which emphasize sustainability and social responsibility, were key drivers of this growth[37][38].

Tesla: Tesla, arguably the poster child for sustainability and profitability, saw its revenue more than double from $31.5 billion in 2020 to $81.5 billion in 2022. Despite the global supply chain issues that hit automakers hard during the pandemic, Tesla's focus on electric vehicles and sustainable energy solutions helped it weather the storm. Tesla became one of the world's most valuable companies, with a market capitalization of over $1 trillion in 2021. The company's alignment with growing consumer demand for cleaner, electric alternatives continues to set it apart from traditional automakers, whose pandemic recovery has been slower[39][40].

Apple: Apple continues to push the envelope on sustainability, aiming to make its entire supply chain carbon neutral by 2030. The company has already reduced its carbon footprint by 40% since 2015, despite seeing revenues increase by 33% in 2021. Apple attributes this in part to eco-conscious consumers who are willing to pay a premium for products made by companies with strong environmental credentials. The company's sustainability efforts have also translated into supply chain efficiencies, saving Apple money while enhancing its reputation as a climate leader[41][42].

Nestlé: Nestlé, the world's largest food and beverage company, launched its Net Zero Roadmap in 2020, pledging to halve its emissions by 2030 and reach net-zero by 2050. Even in the aftermath of the pandemic, Nestlé continued to see positive growth, with an 8.4% increase in sales in 2021. The company's investments in regenerative agriculture and sustainable sourcing, particularly for cocoa and dairy, have helped Nestlé future-proof its supply chains and reduce its environmental impact. This sustainability-first strategy has also improved its reputation among consumers who are increasingly conscious of where their food comes from[43][44].

Ørsted: Ørsted, once a heavily fossil fuel-dependent company, has completely transformed itself into a global leader in renewable energy. As of 2020, Ørsted generated 90% of its energy from renewable sources, compared to just 15% a decade earlier. Ørsted's share price has more than quadrupled since it began its transition, proving that even industries deeply entrenched in fossil fuels can turn things around and achieve profitability through sustainability[45][46].

Companies don't need to be climate activists to

recognize the business case for sustainability. Sustainable practices aren't just about protecting the planet—they're also about protecting profits. From improved efficiency and cost savings to stronger consumer loyalty and regulatory compliance, the data shows that going green is simply good business. When companies incorporate sustainability into their business models, they not only contribute to environmental and social well-being but also position themselves for long-term success.

Key Takeaway: The climate crisis is urgent, and we need imperfect solutions to start driving change. We shouldn't let Gregory Purist's argument for the "perfect" solution stop us from acting. Every step we take—whether it's incentivizing no-till farming, using carbon credits to fund agroforestry, or financing smallholder farmers through Green Bonds—brings us closer to a more sustainable future.

We have the tools—we just need to keep using them, even if they aren't perfect yet. Because in the battle against climate change, progress beats perfection every time. The future of our planet doesn't hinge on finding the perfect solution—it hinges on taking action today. Whether you're a business leader, a farmer, or a consumer, there's a role for you to play. Start small, start imperfectly, but start now. Because when it comes to fighting climate change, every step forward is progress.

11
A Way Forward

So, here we are, the final chapter. We've covered a lot of ground—carbon credits, insets, green bonds, unicorns, Pegasi (Pegasuses? No, that's not right.), and a whole lot of complex global problems. Now it's time to talk about the future. Not some vague, dystopian "we're all doomed" vision of the future but one that's grounded in hope, action, and, dare I say it, optimism.

Let's lay out a roadmap for what an ideal system of sustainable agriculture could look like—one that's inclusive, equitable, and environmentally impactful. This is a vision where smallholder farmers, big corporations, consumers, and governments work in harmony to create a food system that not only sustains us but helps heal the planet. And after we're done singing kumbaya, we'll work on world peace and creating the world's perfect sandwich. But really, just because it seems out of reach, doesn't mean it has to be.

Vision for the Future: An Ideal System of Sustainable Agriculture

Picture this: It's 2040, and agriculture is no longer the

villain in the climate crisis. Instead, it's part of the solution. The ideal system of sustainable agriculture is one that balances the needs of farmers, the economy, and the environment in a way that's beneficial to all. But what does that really mean?

Inclusivity and Equity: In the ideal future, the global agricultural system isn't dominated by a handful of massive, well-capitalized farms, leaving smallholders and marginalized farmers on the sidelines. Instead, smallholder farmers have the tools, knowledge, and financial support to participate fully in sustainable practices. Whether through accessible financing options like microcredit programs or through community-led initiatives, everyone—regardless of geography or resources—has a stake in this new world.

This means more targeted policies and subsidies that directly support small-scale farmers, particularly in the Global South, who are often the most vulnerable to climate change. It means technology and financial instruments that scale down, not just up, making it possible for even the smallest farms to reap the benefits of carbon markets, sustainable certifications, and environmental incentives. It means access to technology, education and training that helps enhance efficiency and productivity. Because technology is supposed to lift us up as a society, not separate us even further (I'm looking at you, social media). It means creating ecosystems of funding, technology, training and markets that are geared to actively support and include women and traditionally marginalized groups to bring encourage and enhance the strength that a diverse labor and business base provides.

Economic Equity: In this future, farmers—especially those in developing countries—are earning a fair share of the value of the crops they grow. They're not just the first link in a long supply chain but active participants in a system that recognizes and rewards their contribution to the food and climate ecosystem.

Carbon insetting schemes, premium market labels, and green bonds ensure that farmers get paid not just for the food they produce but for the environmental services they provide. These sustainable farming practices lead to resilient communities and a more balanced distribution of wealth across the food system. This requires more open and transparent access to markets. The technology for this has existed for more than a decade. Why smallholder farmers still have to rely on middlemen for market access and thus remain at the mercy of their largesse is unfathomable.

Environmental Impact: In the ideal future, farming doesn't just "do less harm"—it actively heals the planet. Through practices like agroforestry, regenerative agriculture, and smart water management systems like Alternate Wetting and Drying (AWD), agriculture sequesters carbon, restores biodiversity, and conserves water. Instead of depleting natural resources, farming regenerates them. Farms become a source of biodiversity that increases overall ecological health and farm yield, helping our pollinators bounce back and improving the resilience of the biome both above and below ground.

Data-driven MRV systems provide transparency, ensuring that sustainability claims are backed by real-world results. Technologies like blockchain track the progress, offering a degree of public trust and accountability that's long overdue.

This vision may sound ambitious, but here's the kicker—it's possible. The tools, technologies, and financial frameworks to make this happen already exist. Unlike many of the super ambitious technology-driven climate solutions being floated around out there, everything we need to make this work already exists...except the will to implement. What we need is the collective will to put them to use.

Ecosystem of Support: How Everyone Can Play Their Part

The beauty of this vision is that it's not a one-person show. It takes a village—a global village. It's not one country, one company or one industry that will make this work. Each stakeholder in the system has a role to play, and when they work together, we get a sustainable agricultural ecosystem that benefits everyone. Here's how different groups can contribute:

Farmers: Farmers, particularly smallholders, are at the heart of this transformation. Their role is to adopt sustainable practices—like no-till farming, agroforestry, or organic farming—that reduce emissions, improve soil health, and enhance biodiversity. But they shouldn't be expected to do this alone. They need access to financial resources, technical training, and market incentives to make these changes sustainable in the long term.

Farmer cooperatives and regional farming groups can help pool resources and share knowledge, making it easier for smaller farms to scale sustainable practices. Governments, NGOs, and the private sector must continue to offer technical support and ensure that farmers are not bearing the full cost of sustainability.

Consumers: Let's face it—consumers hold a lot of power. The choices we make at the grocery store or online checkout shape entire industries. When consumers demand sustainably sourced products, companies respond. This demand can be both active and passive and can snowball quickly into an unstoppable force.

You—yes, you reading this—can drive change by supporting brands and farmers who prioritize sustainability. Look for eco-labels, Fair Trade certifications, or products backed by carbon insetting initiatives. While we can't all live in solar-powered yurts and grow our own kale, small shifts in purchasing habits can signal to companies that sustainability matters. Be vocal about it (without being preachy) and make sure your friends understand why it's important to support sustainably sourced products beyond the environmental impact.

Corporations: Big businesses aren't the villains of this story. In fact, they play a crucial role in scaling sustainable practices. By integrating sustainability into their supply chains, companies can help drive widespread adoption of green practices. Corporations need to continue investing in carbon insetting programs, sourcing sustainable ingredients, and committing to long-term sustainability goals.

Companies can also use their vast financial and technical resources to help farmers transition to more sustainable practices. Programs that provide farmers with financial incentives for adopting sustainability, like Nespresso's AAA Sustainable Quality™ Program, are great examples of how corporations can support farmers while improving their own environmental footprint.

Governments: Policy is the backbone of systemic change. Governments must continue to create and enforce environmental regulations that encourage sustainable practices—whether through subsidies, carbon pricing, or regulatory measures like the EU's Carbon Border Adjustment Mechanism (CBAM). Governments also need to ensure that funding for climate-smart agriculture is accessible to all, not just the biggest players.

Moreover, governments can facilitate the scaling of sustainable practices by funding research, promoting transparency in carbon markets, and building infrastructure that supports sustainable agriculture (think better rural internet access, soil health monitoring systems, and low-interest green loans). I'm generally not a fan of price setting either, but setting a floor for carbon in a system where carbon allowances is limited, makes sense, and is important to ensuring investors have confidence in the financial stability of the entire endeavor, especially at the beginning of the process.

NGOs and International Organizations: NGOs play a critical role in advocating for the most vulnerable players in the system—smallholder farmers, indigenous communities, and women. They can help bridge the gap between farmers and the complex world of sustainability finance, offering training, technical assistance, and even funding.

International organizations, like the World Bank or FAO, should continue to fund large-scale initiatives that promote sustainable agriculture and carbon reduction. These global players can also help develop frameworks that ensure smaller projects are not left behind in the rush to scale up. Private funds like the Bezos Earth Fund, Bill & Melinda Gates Foundation and the Rockefeller Foundation are all working towards a more sustainable future. The 11th Hour Project is another terrific example. It is part of the Schmidt Family Foundation with a key focus on climate change and sustainable agriculture, especially those projects created and run by people from the communities in which the projects operate. Getting this buy-in from project inception is a critical part of ensuring true equity across all parts of the project and something that should be considered a priority whenever possible.

Final Call to Action: Your Role in the Future

Okay, here's the part where I ask for something. But don't worry, I'm not going to guilt-trip you into turning off your air conditioner or selling your car for a bamboo bike. The truth is, everyone has a role to play in shaping a more sustainable future—and it doesn't have to involve radical lifestyle changes.

Maybe you're a consumer who starts choosing products

with eco-labels more frequently, nudging corporations to prioritize sustainable sourcing. Maybe you're a business leader who decides to green your supply chain or invest in sustainable practices. Or maybe you're a farmer who experiments with a regenerative technique like cover cropping.

Regardless of where you sit within the ecosystem, sustainability is a group project. We've got all the tools we need—what's missing is widespread participation. So, here's your part: get involved. Start small, but start somewhere. Make the choice to support companies and policies that prioritize sustainability. Encourage your local community, family, or workplace to think about the long-term impact of their decisions. Don't be afraid to let your elected representative know that the environment should not be a partisan issue. We all have to live here, after all.

I've tried to approach this topic with a bit of levity, but the truth is there's an urgency here. Climate change isn't waiting around for the perfect solution, and neither can we. It doesn't care about your Q3 numbers or your follower count on TikTok. Don't wait for the "right" time to start, because the "right" time was a couple decades ago. Progress doesn't happen in a straight line, and no one is expecting perfection. But every step forward counts. Whether you're a policymaker, an academic, a consumer, a business leader, or a farmer, there's a role for you in this movement.

Final Takeaway

In the battle against climate change and environmental degradation, progress beats perfection every time. So, let's get moving. Whether it's choosing sustainable products, investing in green bonds, or pushing for better government policies, every little action contributes to the broader movement. Together, we can build a food system that's not just sustainable but also equitable and inclusive—one that works for everyone, from smallholder farmers in the Global South to the eco-conscious consumers in the Global North.

In the end, it's not just about saving the planet—it's about building a future where we all thrive.

So, what are you waiting for? Let's get started. After all, the yellow spotted jackalwhompus isn't going to save itself.

APPENDIX
Green Bonds: Financing the Future of Sustainability

Green Bonds have emerged as a powerful tool for financing sustainability projects, including those in agriculture, energy, and carbon reduction. Unlike traditional bonds, which raise capital for general business activities, Green Bonds are earmarked for projects that deliver environmental benefits, such as reducing greenhouse gas emissions, increasing energy efficiency, or promoting sustainable land use. They provide investors with a way to support environmentally friendly initiatives while also earning financial returns, making them a crucial mechanism for financing the transition to a low-carbon economy.

In the context of sustainable agriculture and carbon reduction, Green Bonds are gaining traction as governments and corporations recognize the need to channel significant capital into projects that drive both economic growth and environmental resilience. Let's explore how Green Bonds are being used effectively around the world.

Case Study 1: France's Sovereign Green Bonds

In 2017, France became one of the first countries to issue sovereign Green Bonds, raising €7 billion (about $8.3 billion USD at the time) to fund projects aimed at combatting climate change. A significant portion of these funds was directed toward sustainable agriculture, including projects that promote agroecology, organic farming, and the reduction of chemical inputs. By incentivizing practices that reduce greenhouse gas emissions from farming, France's Green Bond issuance has provided farmers with the financial backing to adopt sustainable techniques, proving that governments can use Green Bonds to support environmental goals on a national scale.

The French government has set a high standard for transparency and reporting, releasing annual reports to investors that detail the environmental impact of the funded projects. This approach has earned France's Green Bonds widespread credibility and investor confidence, creating a model for other nations to follow.

Case Study 2: Chile's Green Bonds for Climate Resilience

Chile made history in 2019 by issuing Latin America's first sovereign Green Bonds, raising $2.5 billion to fund projects aimed at reducing carbon emissions and increasing climate resilience. Among these projects are significant investments in sustainable agriculture, particularly in regions vulnerable to the effects of climate change. Funds have been allocated to water management systems that improve irrigation efficiency, enabling farmers to grow crops with reduced water use, and reduce emissions associated with energy-intensive irrigation practices.

Chile's issuance has been highly successful, with the bonds oversubscribed multiple times, reflecting the strong demand from global investors for environmentally focused financial products. The country has since issued more Green Bonds to scale up its sustainability initiatives, cementing its role as a leader in climate financing in the Global South.

Case Study 3: Rabobank's Green Bond for Sustainable Agriculture

Rabobank, a Dutch multinational banking and financial services company, is one of the world's largest lenders to the agriculture sector. In 2016, Rabobank issued its first Green Bond focused on financing sustainable agriculture projects, raising €500 million (about $588 million USD). The proceeds were used to support Dutch farmers in transitioning to more sustainable farming practices, such as adopting organic farming, reducing the use of synthetic fertilizers, and improving animal welfare standards.

What made Rabobank's Green Bond unique was its focus on the intersection of agriculture and climate action. By financing carbon-reducing practices in farming, the bond aligned financial returns with environmental goals, offering a blueprint for how the private sector can support sustainable agriculture. Rabobank's success has spurred other banks and financial institutions to explore similar models, recognizing the growing demand for Green Bonds that support the food and agriculture sectors.

Case Study 4: Kenya's Green Bond for Renewable Energy in Agriculture

In 2019, Kenya made headlines with the launch of Africa's first Green Bond listed on the London Stock Exchange. Although much of the bond was dedicated to financing renewable energy projects, it also included funding for renewable energy solutions within agriculture, such as solar-powered irrigation systems and biodigesters that convert agricultural waste into energy. These innovations are crucial for smallholder farmers, who often lack access to reliable electricity or affordable energy sources.

Kenya's Green Bond has helped improve both the financial resilience of smallholder farmers and their environmental impact by reducing reliance on fossil fuels. The success of this bond has encouraged other African nations to consider Green Bonds as a way to finance climate-resilient agriculture and other sustainability initiatives.

How Green Bonds Are Transforming Sustainability Financing

Green Bonds are increasingly being recognized as a critical tool in scaling sustainable agriculture and carbon-reduction projects globally. They provide a lower-cost source of capital for projects that might otherwise struggle to attract traditional financing, particularly in developing regions or industries like agriculture, where margins are tight and risks are high.

Key benefits of Green Bonds include:
- Attracting Capital: Investors, particularly those with a focus on Environmental, Social, and Governance (ESG) standards, are drawn to Green Bonds for both their financial returns and their positive environmental impact.
- De-Risking Sustainable Projects: By providing a steady flow of capital to sustainable projects, Green Bonds help de-risk initiatives that may carry higher upfront costs, such as transitioning to low-emission farming methods or installing renewable energy systems in agricultural operations.
- Boosting Transparency: Green Bonds often come with stringent reporting requirements, ensuring that the funds are used for their intended purposes and providing

investors with a clear view of the environmental benefits generated. This boosts credibility and fosters greater trust in carbon markets and sustainability efforts.

- Scaling Up Impact: Governments and corporations alike are using Green Bonds to finance sustainability projects on a large scale. As more capital flows into these bonds, the potential for widespread adoption of sustainable practices increases, providing a scalable solution to some of the world's most pressing environmental challenges.

The Future of Green Bonds in Agriculture and Carbon Reduction

As the demand for climate-smart agriculture and carbon reduction projects continues to grow, the role of Green Bonds is expected to expand. More governments and private sector players are likely to issue Green Bonds dedicated to financing projects that reduce carbon emissions, improve biodiversity, and promote sustainable land use. Emerging markets, in particular, could benefit from these financial instruments, as they seek to attract the capital needed to finance their transitions to more sustainable agricultural systems.

To further enhance the impact of Green Bonds in agriculture, innovative mechanisms such as coupling them with carbon credits or insets could be explored. For instance, by linking the bond's repayment to the generation of carbon credits, issuers can create additional financial incentives for both investors and project developers to prioritize projects that deliver measurable carbon reductions.

Bibliography

(1)   Office of the Assistant Director-General, Natural Resources Management and Environment Department. Smallholders and Family Farmers. Rome, FAO, 2013. 4p.

(2)   FAO Regional Office for Asia and the Pacific. (2021). Impact of Climate Change on Agriculture and Food Security. Food and Agriculture Organization of the United Nations.

(3)   Southeast Asian Climate Consortium. (2021). Farmers' Perceptions of Climate Change in Southeast Asia. Southeast Asian Climate Consortium Reports.

(4)   Asian Development Bank (ADB). (2020). Climate Change and Rural Communities in Southeast Asia: Economic and Environmental Vulnerabilities. Asian Development Bank.

(5)   Geophysical Fluid Dynamics Laboratory. Global Warming and Hurricanes. Princeton, NJ: National Oceanic and Atmospheric Administration (NOAA), 2023.

(6)   Rowan University. New Study Finds 50-Year Trend in Hurricane Escalation Linked to Climate Change. ScienceDaily, October 19, 2023.

(7)   NASA Science. A Force of Nature: Hurricanes in a Changing Climate. NASA, 2023.

(8)   United States Environmental Protection Agency. Climate Change Indicators: Tropical Cyclone Activity. Washington, DC: EPA, 2023.

(9)   Northwest Horticultural Council. "Apple Fact Sheet." Northwest Horticultural Council, 2024.

(10)   Washington State University Tree Fruit Research & Extension Center. "2015 Washington State Apple Crop Report: Effects of High Temperatures and Water Stress on Apple Quality and Yield." Washington State University, 2016.

(11)   Intergovernmental Panel on Climate Change (IPCC). "Fact Sheet: Food and Water." Sixth Assessment Report, Working Group II – Impacts, Adaptation and Vulnerability.

(12)   World Bank. "Making Climate Finance Work in Agriculture." World Bank Group, 2024.

(13)   Food and Agriculture Organization of the United Nations. "Climate Change and Food Security: Risks and Responses." FAO, 2016.

(14)   International Food Policy Research Institute. "Global Food Policy Report 2019." IFPRI, 2019.

(15)   World Bank. "Agriculture Overview: Development News, Research, Data." World Bank Group, 2024.

(16)   World Bank. "The Future of Food: Shaping the Global Food System to Deliver Improved Nutrition and Health." World Bank, 2021.

(17)   Food and Agriculture Organization of the United Nations (FAO). "Unlocking Finance for African Smallholder Farmers." FAO, 2023.

(18)   Food and Agriculture Organization of the United Nations (FAO). "Africa's Smallholder Farmers." FAO, 2010.

(19)   United States Department of Agriculture (USDA). Task Force on Agriculture and Rural Prosperity Report. Washington, DC: USDA, 2018.

(20)   American Diabetes Association (ADA). "Economic Costs of Diabetes in the U.S. in 2017." Diabetes Care, 2018.

(21)   American Heart Association (AHA). "Cardiovascular Disease: A Costly Burden for America—Projections through 2035." American Heart Association, 2017.

(22)   National Heart, Lung, and Blood Institute (NHLBI), NIH. "Americans' Poor Diet Drives $50 Billion a Year in

Health Care Costs." NHLBI in the Press, 2019.

(23)   Lal, R. (2020). "Regenerative Agriculture for Climate Change Mitigation and Adaptation." Journal of Soil and Water Conservation, 75(5), 123A-127A.

(24)   Gerber, P. J., et al. (2013). "Tackling climate change through livestock: A global assessment of emissions and mitigation opportunities." Food and Agriculture Organization of the United Nations (FAO).

(25)   Smith, P., et al. (2016). "The role of soils in delivering Nature's Contributions to People: carbon storage and climate regulation." Nature, 540, 53-61.

(26)   World Resources Institute. (2015). Farmer-Managed Natural Regeneration: A Success in Sustainable Land Management in Niger.

(27)   European Environment Agency. (2020). Trends and projections in Europe 2020: Tracking progress towards Europe's climate and energy targets.

(28)   Manley, B. (2020). The New Zealand Emissions Trading Scheme: Critical Review and Future Outlook. New Zealand Journal of Forestry Science.

(29)   Nespresso. (2018). The Positive Cup: AAA Sustainable Quality Program – Annual Review

(30)   Clark, G., Feiner, A., & Viehs, M. (2015). From the stockholder to the stakeholder: How sustainability can drive financial outperformance. University of Oxford and Arabesque Partners.

(31)   Nielsen (2019). The Evolution of the Sustainability Mindset. Nielsen.

(32)   McKinsey & Company (2021). The decarbonization challenge: How business is rising to the occasion.

(33)   Eccles, R. G., Ioannou, I., & Serafeim, G. (2014).

The Impact of Corporate Sustainability on Organizational Processes and Performance. Management Science, 60(11), 2835-2857.

(34)   Bloomberg Intelligence (2021). ESG assets may hit $53 trillion by 2025, a third of global AUM.

(35)   Microsoft (2021). Microsoft will be carbon negative by 2030. Microsoft.

(36)   CNBC (2021). Microsoft's carbon negative pledge hasn't hurt its stock performance. CNBC.

(37)   Unilever (2021). Climate action and social commitments drive business success. Unilever.

(38)   Unilever (2021). Full Year Results 2021. Unilever.

(39)   Tesla (2022). Tesla, Inc. Q4 2022 Update. Tesla.

(40)   CNBC (2021). Tesla tops $1 trillion in market value, joining Apple, Microsoft, Amazon, Google parent Alphabet. CNBC.

(41)   Apple (2021). Apple commits to being 100 percent carbon neutral for its supply chain and products by 2030. Apple.

(42)   Apple (2022). Apple financial results. Apple.

(43)   Nestlé (2020). Nestlé accelerates action to tackle climate change and commits to net zero emissions by 2050. Nestlé.

(44)   Nestlé (2021). Nestlé 2021 Full Year Results. Nestlé.

(45)   Ørsted (2021). Ørsted to become carbon neutral by 2025. Ørsted.

(46)   The Guardian (2020). How Denmark's Ørsted went from black to green energy. The Guardian.

ACKNOWLEDGEMENTS

A significant amount of time went into the research and writing of this book and that time came at the expense of many evenings and late dinners. So, I'd first like to thank my wife and children for their patience, support and understanding during this process. Courtney, your tireless efforts to keep the wheels from falling off cannot be adequately recognized in this short paragraph, but thank you.

I'd also be remiss not to thank my partners and co-founders at Spiro Carbon for their support. Dr. Ammarin Daranpob was, and always has been, a great resource for ensuring I don't say stupid things. Dr. Ahmed Mahgoub continually makes me look like I know what I'm talking about in all things tech-related. And David Rockwood is always there to provide support and encouragement, whether or not there's justification for either.

A special thanks goes out to the faculty, staff and administration of the College of Agriculture and Environmental Science at the University of Georgia. Having firsthand access to experts at the best college of agriculture in the country (no disrespect intended to the other fine institutions of learning, but Go Dawgs) has made my overall growth in the sector for the past decade+ much greater than I probably had any right to receive. I would also like to thank the men and women of the UGA Agricultural Cooperative Extension Service. Although I did not receive help from them in the writing of this book, the work they do every day to support the farmers and other citizens of the state of Georgia is incredible and a service to us all.

It's important, I believe, to look at the climate situation

through a lens that recognizes the business realities in addition to the scientific challenges. Addressing climate change is crucial for all of the reasons you hear about most in the media. But it is equally critical because of the long-term economic impact. Being able to see this as not just a challenge, but as an opportunity requires a different perspective. That business-first perspective has been fostered for me by several business mentors who deserve a great deal of thanks as well. Mark Moore, Steve Strout, and Darrin Austin are among the most prolific of these mentors although there have been many others. Thank you for your investment and faith in me, even when neither were necessarily justified or "wise" in the traditional sense.

Finally, I would like to thank the farmers of the world. You come in all shapes and sizes with different ideas and motivations, but the truth is, we wouldn't be here without you. Through you, I have been given a glimpse of the immense challenge we face but also the hope of a brighter future. Because of all the populations in the world, few are as resilient, tough, smart and determined as a farmer. You represent the potential of what we can achive. My hope is that I have helped make your case just a little bit in this book and that the governments, corporations and consumers of the world, can rally behind you to help make you the tip of the spear in creating a stronger, more sustainable future for everyone.

Every effort was made in the writing of this book to be accurate and objective. But I'm as far from perfect as one can get and still capable of functioning mostly like an adult. So, any errors found within the pages here are wholly mine and not due to any information, advice or guidance received by any of the companies, individuals or organizations referenced in the book. Thank you for reading this. Now go do something to help.

ABOUT THE AUTHOR

Benjamin Worley is a lifelong entrepreneur who has spent the last decade and change working in the agriculture and environmental technology sector. His work has taken him around the world, deploying solutions on more than 1 million hectares in 14 countries on 4 continents. Ben is a frequent speaker at international events related to sustainability and sustainable finance including the UN's COP28, UN SDG Labs during the World Economic Forum, Abu Dhabi Sustainable Finance Week, Dubai Fintech Summit, and many other conferences and events. He has helped design and develop novel solutions in the artificial intelligence, remote sensing, GIS and blockchain technology sectors related to agriculture and sustainability. Ben is also the co-inventor on multiple patents related to AI and has been the CEO of two startups in AgTech and ClimateTech. Ben and his family live in Georgia, splitting their time between their home just north of Atlanta and the family farm in the mountains of North Georgia.

www.ingramcontent.com/pod-product-compliance
Lightning Source LLC
Chambersburg PA
CBHW052316220526
45472CB00001B/150